MODERN ARCHITECTURE

IN BRAZIL

Henrique E. Mindlin

MODERN ARCHITECTURE IN BRAZIL

PREFACE BY PROF. S. GIEDION

THE ARCHITECTURAL PRESS LONDON

Published in English language edition

for the USA and Canada REINHOLD PUBLISHING CORPORATION, *New York*

for the British Commonwealth except Canada THE ARCHITECTURAL PRESS, *London*

for South America LIVRARIA KOSMOS EDITORA, *Rio de Janeiro*

for all other countries MEULENHOFF & CO N V, *Amsterdam*

French edition

for France and Italy VINCENT, FRÉAL & CIE, *Paris*

German edition

for Germany, Switzerland and Austria VERLAG GEORG D. W. CALLWEY, *Munich*

to the memory of my father Dr E. H. Mindlin

friend of the arts and of artists

ODESSA, RUSSIA, 9 IX 1886—SANTOS, BRAZIL, 12 III 1939

BRAZIL AND CONTEMPORARY ARCHITECTURE

It is a good sign for our civilization that it is spreading from more than one center. Creative work suddenly appears in countries which in earlier periods would have remained provincial. Finland and Brazil: how is it possible that these countries that have been lying for such a long time on the outskirts of civilization show such a high architectural standard? What is the reason? Is it the architects? No doubt, without creative architects there can be no creative work, but creative architects exist in many other countries. What is lacking in many other countries, however, is the financial support and the clients, governments and administrations which do not hamper real talent. The trouble in present day architecture is due to the fact that the backbone of the architect, in dictatorial as well as in democratic states, is broken by the taste of the clients. Finland and Brazil are two countries in which this is not the case. No misdirected resistance on the part of the clients is killing the creative impulse. And it has become apparent during the last twenty years that in the Tropics as well as near the Polar Circle the ground is ready for a new development, if only it is not spoilt artificially.

Brazil: a very interesting problem of a long dormant culture. More than 400 years ago, not far from present day Santos, the first city was founded in 1532. Brazil constituted an agrarian society. The planters lived with priest and chapel in their own houses; they exploited the country, but also created cultural treasures on the basis of extensive farming. Indians with bows and arrows, negroes with muskets formed a body-guard for the masters. As a class the landowners formed a free society, ready at all times to resist the incursions of Crown or Church. It has been said by Gilberto Freyre that the Portuguese were the first Europeans who placed the family and not the trading company in the center of civilization.

In contrast to the United States, the Portuguese have carried on their tradition of mixing with other races. It was Count Keyserling who pointed out the unity in Brazil, in spite of racial differences. Unlike the USA, Brazil has solved the difficult racial problem: in the beautiful housing estates of Pedregulho negroes and Norwegians are living side by side.
There is another problem, which to the foreigner seems to be an enormous handicap to the internal peace and the future of Brazil. This is the reckless speculation in land. It is the cancer of Brazilian development. Unless it is reduced drastically, Brazil will certainly be able to produce fine architecture, but it will be menaced ceaselessly by the tremors of political upheaval.

Brazil is a country of contrasts, product of a hectic period of speculation. Primitive huts are spreading like mushrooms in the no-man's land of the great cities or are built on ridiculously high priced ground on their outskirts. No equilibrium in the social structure and in town planning in the widest sense can be achieved before the financial chaos is overcome.
Amidst this the wonder of Brazilian architecture is spreading like a tropical plant. Brazil has comparatively little iron and cement industry. Yet everywhere skyscrapers are shooting up. There is something irrational in the rise of Brazilian architecture. In contrast to the USA with its sequence of great precursors since the 1880's—Richardson, Louis Sullivan, F. L. Wright—Brazil is finding its own architectural expression with an astonishing rapidity. Of course when Le Corbusier came to Brazil in 1936 it was the spark which kindled talents to find their own way of expression.

But Le Corbusier had been in many other countries and it very often led to nothing or to nasty headlines as once in the New York newspapers.

Modern architecture in Brazil by Henrique Mindlin—a noted architect in his country—serves a valuable purpose by opening the eyes of the outer world to the contemporary architecture that has arisen in Brazil. He has handled his subject in a very straight-forward way, both in his introduction and, especially, in his brief, *objective* explanations accompanying the many illustrations.
In Brazil, contemporary architecture is rooted in the tropical Brazilian soil. It shot up at a moment when many large architectural projects were being undertaken. Relations with the regional past were never cut off. But Henrique Mindlin also stresses the outstanding importance for later developments of the one month's visit of Le Corbusier in 1936, during which he worked with a group of young Brazilian architects. Among the reasons for the close relations that were established between them may have been their common Latin background. Another probable reason was the ready employment in Brazil of ferro-concrete as the structural material for large buildings. This is in sharp contrast to the development in the United States, where large scale architecture has been based on the use of structural steel.
The efflorescence of Brazilian architecture since the late thirties is evident from Henrique Mindlin's book. Our special interest is drawn to *the most recent development in the fifties*—much of which has remained unknown outside his own country. In this way it has now become possible to compare the work of contemporary Brazilian architects with standards and trends in other parts of the world. With what result?
First one has to recognize that in Brazil a certain standard of achievement is maintained throughout. While certain characteristics may be especially apparent in the work of outstanding individuals, they are also evident in the average level of architectural production: a situation that does not exist in most other countries. To give a few instances: most Brazilian architects seem able to tackle the varied problems of a complex program and to come forward with a concise and simple ground plan and with clear and intelligent sections.
Brazilian architects also have the courage to develop clearcut lines in the exterior of their buildings. They know how to avoid roughness, a danger which certain other countries in their hemisphere did not escape.
Thirdly, while from the earliest days wall surfaces in Brazil—under the pressure of tropical conditions—have been enlivened by a structural treatment of the plain surfaces, contemporary architects have now elaborated this tradition to include hollowed exterior panels (page 58), pierced tile work (Lúcio Costa's Bristol apartments, since 1948), new uses of ceramic tiles, and the *brise-soleil*. This treatment of wall surfaces in Brazil is related to a general trend that has more recently become evident elsewhere.
Their handling of interior space is often of interest too. Besides the skyscraper chaos in Rio and São Paulo, we have seen the results of an inherent gift to connect volumes of space (e.g. Reidy's Pedregulho development, since 1951, page 120, and Niemeyer's Aeronautical center, 1947, page 112), especially in recent manifestations, such as the domed Palace of the Arts by Oscar Niemeyer and others, designed for sculpture exhibitions. In this case the main interest lies in the perforation of the interior space through three levels, below and above the ground.
We expect that in the very near future Brazilian architects will

play their part in the task of evolving the vaulted form of our own period. We are today in the process of discovering the specific form of the vault of our time which is different from that of *all* foregoing periods. This is not the place to discuss it. I have made some comments upon the direction in which we are moving in my small booklet *Architektur und Gemeinschaft* (Hamburg, 1956), in my analysis of the work of Eduardo Catalano, Hugh Stubbins' Conference Hall for Berlin, 1957, and Le Corbusier's pilgrimage church at Ronchamp, which give perhaps the clearest indications of the lines along which I believe the solution will be found.

How is all this related to nature in the environment in which it is taking place, with its tropical growth that one can almost feel bodily? Brazil has given us also Burle Marx, one of the few great landscape architects. He is a painter. What can we learn from him? His is the application of horizontal structural surfaces. Often simple plants are chosen, such as grow in our own countries: for instance the so-called day-lilies. They are assembled in curved, very often kidney-shaped flower beds, forming large yellow and orange colored surfaces; an example of this is to be found in the garden of Henrique Mindlin's summer house (page 37). This is a principle of organization transposed from the pictures of modern painters into living nature.

I hope that this book will help the world to get a better insight into what happened in Brazil during the two most important decades of its architectural development.

Zurich, Doldertal, May 1956

S. GIEDION

CONTENTS

AUTHOR'S NOTE

This work was first begun as a supplement to *Brazil Builds*, Philip L. Goodwin's superlatively well written presentation of old and new architecture in Brazil, published by the Museum of Modern Art of New York, and illustrated with splendid photographs by G. E. Kidder Smith. However, since *Brazil Builds* has been out of print for quite a few years now, it was later decided to include here the most important examples already shown in that book. In this way a more complete picture may be given, covering the development of modern architecture in Brazil since its beginning in the late twenties up to our days. But it does not replace Goodwin's beautiful job, nor was it ever my intention that it did so.

The purpose of this book is rather to provide, in as condensed and orderly a manner as possible, by means of a number of selected examples, a picture of what Brazil has achieved in the way of modern architecture, in order that a substantiated appraisal may be undertaken, both by the architects themselves and by honest critics here and abroad.

The need to cover a large territory in a set number of pages imposed many limitations in the choice of the material to be presented. A great many good projects had to be excluded, especially when their most relevant points were shown in other jobs already illustrated. As it goes to press, the author and the publishers hope that attention will be called to its faults and errors, so that they may be corrected in further printings.

I should like, however, to express here my deep indebtedness to all who have helped me so far, and who are not to be blamed for such faults: to Vera, without whose wifely forbearance, and willing sacrifice of all our leisure time I should never have finished this book; to Walmyr Lima Amaral, Samuel Levy, Anny Sirakoff, Olga Verjovsky, Marcos Demetre Foundoukas and Sergio Campos, of my office, who helped organize, classify and prepare the material for publication; to Fernando Tabora, João Távora, Herman Neves Apostolo, Jayme de Gouveia Veloso, Jayme Leal, Wilson Azevedo Sergio, José Lopes Pires, Roberto Radler de Aquino, also of my office, who assisted in its preparation; to Jorge Picorelli, who helped us out with drawings urgently needed when the office force was unavailable for that purpose; to Zilda Ribeiro Bueno Ferreira, my patient secretary, who must have typed and re-typed these pages a million times, and who kept nagging all the architects in order to avoid unseemly delays; to my colleagues who helped me obtain indispensable material, especially Renato Soeiro, Carmen Portinho, Lygia Fernandes and Giancarlo Palanti, as well as J. Faria Góes, Marcos Jaimovich, José Simeão Leal, Oscar Ciampiglia, and Antonio Joaquim de Almeida; to Lota de Macedo Soares, who let me use the wonderful study in her Samambáia house; to Elizabeth Bishop, who put into shape the Portuguese original for the introductory text and for the first comments on individual examples, taking time out which would have been better used in her own writing, since her poetry brought her in 1956 the Pulitzer Poetry Award; to John Knox, who went through an agonizing process translating the large remaining text; to Marcel Gautherot, Jean Manzon, Leon Liberman, Mary Shand and all the other photographers whose beautiful pictures will save the day for this book; to Mr. and Mrs. Finn Engersen, Mr. and Mrs. Alan Fisher, and Mr. Ronald Bottrall, for many suggestions and comments; to Lúcio Costa, Mário Pedrosa, Mário Barata, Hernani Tavares de Sá, Wladimir Alves de Souza and William Atkin for the patient reading of the text, as well as for many corrections; to Claude Vincent for the texts on Roberto Burle Marx's gardens; to Rodrigo Mello Franco de Andrade and to Carlos Drummond de Andrade, for important source material; to KLM Royal Dutch Airlines, for help in the transportation of irreplaceable material; and last, but definitely not least, to Walter Geyerhahn, at whose instigation this book was written, to Osmar Castro, for his layout, even if only partly followed in the final printing job, and to all those whose names cannot be singled simply because too much space would be required.

H. E. M.

MODERN ARCHITECTURE IN BRAZIL

The story of modern architecture in Brazil is the story of a handful of young men and of a body of work brought into existence with incredible rapidity. In a few years,—not even, as might be thought, in a generation, but almost within the turn-over of one school class—an idea which barely had time to take root in São Paulo and Rio de Janeiro had flowered and reached a paradoxical maturity. In his essay on Brazilian architecture [1], Lúcio Costa, whose role in this story can hardly be over-estimated, could say quite truthfully, referring to the period 1930–1940, prior to the building of the Ministry of Education and Health in Rio de Janeiro: 'Never before has architecture passed through such a transformation in such a short period of time.' There was not enough time for the emergence of men like Wright, Berlage and Perret, who had devoted long lives to work and research. In those ten years, in Brazil, International Architecture became Brazilian architecture. This phenomenal development, rooted as it was in the historical events that had brought about the conditions favorable to its growth, appeared nevertheless as an unforseen mutation, not to be accounted for by the inevitabilities of determinism. Its causes must therefore be sought in the intellectual and spiritual preparedness of the national frame of mind. However it came about, it cannot be explained as a mere consequence of the evolution of the art of building in Brazil, or of the country's industrial development.

It should be remembered that the entire history of Brazil covers only four and a half centuries. The transitions from the conquest of a wilderness to the rise of rural patriarchy, from the first semblances of town life to the appearance of cities, and from the comparative security of a slave-holding society to the disruptive impact of industrial revolution, were all accomplished in a fairly short period of time. As a result, the changes in building style reflect the constant social and historical changes, through the epic of the colonization of Portuguese America to the heights of Empire and to the new Republic on its way to becoming a great industrial civilization. The country's need to adapt itself to different ways and conditions of life has naturally left its mark on the history of Brazilian architecture and must have contributed, at least in part, to its fluidity, to the mental elasticity and lack of awe in the face of purely formal tradition, which made possible the abrupt and complete transformation in our time summarized by Lúcio Costa's phrase.

In 1500 the Portuguese discoverer found only the primitive huts of the Indians. But he had brought with him his share of a living culture then at its highest point of energy, and he soon set about transplanting it to the rich and varied land he had conquered. Within four years the first house of stone and mortar was built in Rio de Janeiro [2]. In less than a century some villages had become towns of hundreds of houses, built as much as possible in the Portuguese way. Churches, monasteries, fortresses, and government buildings were gradually scattered along a coastline that finally extended for five thousand miles (the coastline of the Portugal the colonizers had left behind was five hundred miles long). The growth of the private house kept step with the growth of the classes that ruled the colonies: first, in the north, the houses of the sugar cane cultivators appeared; later, to the south, in São Paulo, those of the planters who followed on the march of the *bandeiras* (the ruthless expeditions in search of Indian slaves, and gold and emeralds, which won so much land for Brazil), and in the state of Minas Gerais ('General Mines') those of the wealthy miners. The patriarchal 'big house' was the symbol of a rural aristocracy, a small, autonomous feudal-like domain, bringing together around

the main house the slave quarters, chapel, kitchens, a separate guest room for the occasional traveler, — all the elements essential to as self-sufficient a way of life as possible in the lonely immensities of the new continent. Men were brought from across the sea: later on, African slaves by the thousands and European artisans: materials, too, such as the famous blue and white Portuguese tiles *(azulejos)* and even building stones, since the colonizers were unused to the idea of building with wood. Labor and materials were added to the native resources and little by little a technique suited to the scanty and rudimentary means of the colony was formed. The French and Dutch invaders, during their brief and insecure tenure of Portuguese territory, contributed something of their own national building styles. For example, the two-story building, which had first appeared in Salvador (Bahia) as a result of a growing city

Santa Maria Fort, Salvador, Bahia; Completed in 1696, during the governorship of D. João de Lencastre

aristocracy, seems to have taken on, farther to the north, in Recife under the Dutch, a special character: more dense, compact and vertical: possibly an echo of the tall, narrow, waterfront houses of Holland.

The towns grew up in a rather disorderly way around the churches, which were usually placed on the highest available ground. The streets and by-ways, perhaps under remote Moorish influence, branched and twisted; if they adapted themselves to the lay of the land better than the monotonous checkerboard or gridiron towns laid out by the Spaniards in the rest of South and Central America, they did not embody more than the merest outline of a city-planning scheme. Nevertheless, restrictions were gradually placed on the complete individualism of the 'big house'. The street, that to begin with was no more than the free space beyond the big house and its outbuildings, in the general interest of the community began to impose limitations of its own in return. Before the end of the seventeenth century municipal legislation enacted in Bahia[3], for example, was already disciplining the egocentricity of the house-owner by aligning his house with that of his neighbors', and curbing his tendency to exaggerate the overhang of his balconies and to lower them to the point of endangering the heads of the passers-by. If under the circumstances the building problems of houses and, in a general way, of towns, were solved by normal utilitarianism, those of the churches, built with a fervor lost in our days, gave the native imagination wider scope. In them a characteristic 'Brazilian' note first appeared: in their ingenious interpretations of the inherited canons of architecture, in the never-to-be-surpassed carved wood and gold-and-silver richness of their interiors, and in the skilful integration of sculpture and architecture. The genius of a

São Francisco Church, Salvador, Bahia; Construction begun in 1708, under the direction of Manoel Quaresma, master workman

Santo Alexandre Church, Belém, Pará; Completed 1718–19

new people, bearing signs of the colony's mingling races, began to make its own contribution to the history of art. The appealing if shadowy figure of the 'Aleijadinho', ('The Little Cripple,' Antônio Francisco Lisbôa, 1730–38?–1814) stands out among others, known and unknown, as the one who crystallized the poetic feeling of the new race in his work as sculptor and architect. His twelve Prophets, in front of the Church of Nosso Senhor do Bom Jesus at Congonhas do Campo (Minas Gerais), may seem frozen in the last gauche attitudes of Portuguese baroque; nevertheless, they are authentic, colloquial, and still moving works of art.

By the early nineteenth century a style of building clearly related to its materials had been worked out and, because of the social and economic conditions, had attained the utmost technical simplicity. Within the primitive means at the master workman's disposal, in buildings where circumstances permitted something more exalted than a house of *taipa* or *pau-a-pique* (wattle and adobe, see page 32), and in which a more erudite architecture was already taking the place of traditional popular architecture, a style had been defined, severe, solid, and unadorned. It well expressed the severe and clear-cut social structure: the supremacy of man, the almost-oriental seg-regation of woman, and, supporting the whole, the exploitation of the Negro and the Indian. Perhaps its most remarkable feature was its uniformity throughout the colony, paralleling the remarkable uniformity of language, existing then as now, in such a vast territory with so few lines of communication [4]. Even in the re-ligious architecture, where the hand of an architect and the marks of a training still under baroque influence can most often be felt, a fundamental sobriety underlay the formal exuberance of outline and decoration. Another factor, adaptation to changing conditions, was reflected in almost every detail. There is, for example, the story of the attempted abolition in Bahia and Rio de Janeiro, by

violent decree, of the lattice-work shutters of the colonial house at the beginning of the nineteenth century—an attempt which may have started the fight against the segregation of women, against their virtual imprisonment in the interiors of the houses and their isolation from the life outside its walls. [5]

In 1808 the vicissitudes in the history of the mother country had already had unexpected repercussions in the colony of Brazil. Fleeing before the Napoleonic onslaught, the Prince Regent of Portugal, later Dom João VI, arrived in Rio de Janeiro. In 1809 the Court was installed in Rio, which since 1763 had become, instead of Bahia, the capital of Brazil. An artificial and super-vised Europeanization was hurriedly introduced into a provincial capital, backward and primitive. In 1816, Napoleon having vanished from the scene, a mission of French sculptors, painters, and architects, headed by Lebreton, a painter, was invited to undertake the formal instruction of Brazil in the arts, under the civilizing influence of France. The architect Auguste-Henri-Victor Grandjean de Montigny (1776–1850) became the first professor of architecture at the new Imperial Academy. He was the author of a classic work on the Tuscan order [6], and a capable practising architect, whose designs for the buildings of the Imperial Academy of Fine Arts, the Market Place and the Customs House, among others,—all destroyed now except the Customs House—were mod-els of simple, well-proportioned neo-classic style. His personality molded more than one generation of architects and his influence was indirectly felt for many decades.

But this new and alien movement, completely rootless, boasting a history and a culture very different from the Portuguese, could not help but be a disintegrating force. The art of building in Brazil was split in two. On one side, building of Portuguese origin, but bearing a genuinely 'native' stamp, went on; and on the other,

São Francisco de Assis Church, Ouro Preto, Minas Gerais, Built 1766–94 (attributed to the Aleijadinho)

Detail of Main Altar, São Francisco de Assis Church, Ouro Preto, Minas Gerais, Antônio Francisco Lisbôa, the Aleijadinho

under the regulating and rationalizing French influence, a more erudite and sophisticated architecture appeared. Trained artisans from Europe, like the Germans who arrived in Recife in 1839, and other distinguished architects, such as L. L. Vauthier, who came to Pernambuco in 1840, brought refinement in technique. But none of this could stave off the decadence determined by its nature or circumstance; that is, by the outcome implicit in all academicism, or by the further split, which occurred in Europe as well, caused by the shifting of interests and, later, the new requirements occasioned by the industrial revolution.

In Brazil, which had proclaimed itself independent of Portugal in 1822, official and academic architecture (that is, public buildings and buildings for the use of the wealthier class) was developing along lines increasingly remote from reality. As was bound to happen considering its original imitative nature, it went on its way copying indiscriminately from the most diverse models. After the middle of the nineteenth century the styles in Brazil include, as elsewhere, 'the modest Tuscan', 'the imposing Gothic', 'the handsome Moorish', or 'the elegant chalet', and so on. [7] Art Nouveau was introduced in the larger cities very early in this century, appearing as a sort of architectural protest (however derivative) that was its own justification. Victor Dubugras (1868–1934), again a Frenchman, was the architect who best exploited its possibilities. Its abuse, seen in so many buildings still in existence, was however its logical outcome. This protest, therefore, was bound later to take the form it did in Brazil: that of a neo-colonial reaction that was thought by many to be a return to the one and only legitimate tradition [8]. If to less clear-headed architects it led to a new series of pastiches, for others, such as Lúcio Costa, it rapidly clarified the problem, leading them to take up again the tradition of building closest to Brazilian reality, the only one which, because of its

straightforward response to the climate, the materials, and the needs of the people, could serve as a base and point of departure for a constructive interpretation of the Brazilian architectural requirements in the postwar twentieth century.

This tradition was the one of which the master workmen had become the trustees, keeping it alive throughout the nineteenth century, alongside the sophisticated work of the architects of the French Mission and their followers: a tradition of common sense, balance, and constant change to suit the everchanging conditions of a country still in the formative stage. This tradition, or rather, the spiritual attitude it reflected, brought to self-awareness by the ideas advanced by Le Corbusier, whose work focuses all contemporary achievements, was the one which served as the foundation for the modern architecture movement in Brazil. Le Corbusier's ideas (and to a lesser degree those of Gropius, Van der Rohe and Wright) produced a stimulating trauma that gave it vigor and direction. The personal character it soon took on, distinguishing it from similar movements in Europe and North America, was also found in this tradition.

In the formation of the new movement, from the present point of view, two events, one cultural and one political, stand out as the principal points of reference, producing the conditions favorable to its appearance and its wide acceptance by the general public: the Modern Art Week held in São Paulo in 1922, and the revolution of 1930, which enforced a new regime that affected all levels of administrative, social and economic life of the country.

A hundred years after the proclamation of Independence, Modern Art Week came as another proclamation, one of spiritual revolt. It burst like a bombshell in the parnassian and academic, but highly individualistic, atmosphere of São Paulo. Attacking the old pre-

Interior Detail, Conceição Church, Sabará, Minas Gerais

conceptions and the prevailing eclecticism, in an exhibition of daring 'avant-garde' painting and sculpture and in a series of lectures, dance and music recitals, all held at the stately Municipal Theatre, it loudly announced the 'spirit of the new age'. But, after all, it, too, was a European importation. Perhaps the issues could not be clearly defined by the simple opposition of the terms 'past-ism' and 'futurism',—a 'futurism' that was not really that of the Italian Marinetti, but a mixture of everything new and at hand. But Modern Art Week did give rise to an authentic renaissance which later established a relationship with the highest values of Brazilian life, the sources of the past, the land, and the people. At first, however, extreme movements quickly sprang up, in the eagerness for an independent and national expression, and a further liberation from European influences by means of the artistic creation of Brazil. One of these was the 'anthropophagist' movement of 1928, which tried to find, in the aboriginal culture before the coming of the Portuguese, a spontaneity purified of any 'civilizing' superimposition whatever, Portuguese or European in general. [9] Architecture very soon felt the results of the impact of Modern Art Week. In 1925, Gregori Warchavchik brought out in São Paulo and Rio newspapers [10] his 'Manifesto of Functional Architecture', quoting Le Corbusier's famous slogan, that the house was 'a machine for living', and Rino Levi, then still a student in Rome, published an article in the '*Estado de São Paulo*' (the same newspaper that three years before had announced: 'the columns of this paper are open to all those who by attacking Modern Art Week wish to defend our artistic heritage'), in which he demanded that Brazilian conditions be considered in the urgently needed city planning. A competition was held in 1927 for projects for the Government Palace of the State of São Paulo and Flavio de Carvalho scandalized the public with his 'modernistic' design for a Palace provided with an air-raid shelter. In 1928 Warchavchik showed his first modern house, which attracted thousands of curious visitors and drew upon itself the wrath of the professors.

So that when Le Corbusier first stopped over in São Paulo and Rio de Janeiro on his return from Argentina and Uruguay in 1929, he found the ground more or less prepared. He gave several lectures and in São Paulo he was officially received in the Municipal Chamber with ceremonious speeches and seated at the President's rostrum as an illustrious visitor, all of which appears to have made a strong impression on him. [11] The President-elect, Júlio Prestes, well informed about Le Corbusier's activities, discussed with him the urbanization work he was planning to undertake.

In 1930, however, the revolution led by Getúlio Vargas imposed a new regime and a new state of mind. The 'movement of '30' was made up mostly of young men, both military and civilian, and it produced upheaval and fresh starts in social and economic life as well as in politics.

Repercussions of this period of change and excitement were naturally felt in the field of architecture. The directorship of the National School of Fine Arts in Rio de Janeiro was given to Lúcio Costa, who started overhauling the curriculum, modeled on the *École des Beaux Arts*, from top to bottom. Gregori Warchavchik and A. Budeus were asked to take over the Chairs of Fourth and Fifth year Architectural Design. But Lúcio Costa's reform was never really put into effect. A classroom incident gave the reactionary elements the opportunity to dismiss the young director in less than a year. A strike took place, at first unimportant, but students went on to turn it into a defense of the new artistic ideas, and finally they attempted to found an independent school of their own. The strike lasted six months and when the students returned to their classes they had won a victory for anti-academicism and progress in the arts. In the group of future architects who went through

Prophet in front of Nosso Senhor do Bom Jesus de Matosinhos Church, Congonhas do Campo, Minas Gerais, 1800–04, Antônio Francisco Lisbôa

Old rooftops, São Luis, Maranhão, late XVIII*th and early* XIX*th century*

this period, surely the 'heroic' period of Brazilian architecture, and who had the support of the absolute majority of the student body, were Luiz Nunes (whose premature death cut short a most promising career), Jorge Machado Moreira, Renato Vilela, Carlos Leão, Anníbal de Mello Pinto, Ernani Mendes de Vasconcellos, Orlando Dourado, Raul Marques de Azevedo, Mário Camargo de Penteado, Edison Nicoll, José Carvalho de Castilhos, Regina Reis, Galdino Duprat da Costa Cunha Lima, Antônio Osório Jordão de Brito, José Regis dos Reis, Benedito de Barros, Alcides Rocha Miranda, Ary Garcia Roza, João Lourenço da Silva, Lauro Barboza Coelho, Eugênio da Proença Sigaud, Aldo Garcia Roza, Antônio Pinto, Ruy Costa, Francisco Saturnino de Brito and Edgard Guimarães do Valle. They were first led by Luiz Nunes and then by Jorge Machado Moreira. Later these men helped back up the demands of the students who came after them at the National School.

Nevertheless, the resistance to the new ideas naturally slowed down their being put into practice and the more advanced architects found very few opportunities for work. Then the course of events was interrupted by the Constitutionalist Revolution of 1932 in São Paulo, and only in 1934 was work begun on the building enterprises of the Vargas regime. In 1935 the first studies for Rio de Janeiro's University City were made. In the same year a competition for a new building for the Ministry of Education and Health was announced. In the atmosphere of general artistic hesitancy, the prizes were awarded to purely academic projects, while works of real merit in the modern spirit by a group of young men were disqualified. But then came one of those unexpected happenings that so often change the course of history. The Minister of Education, Gustavo Capanema, inspired by the mixture of vision, audacity and common sense that characterized him, made the personal decision that has contributed most to the development of modern architecture in Brazil. Supported by the opinion of several reputable critics, chiefly Mario de Andrade, Carlos Drummond de Andrade, Rodrigo Melo Franco de Andrade and Manuel Bandeira, as well as that of M. Piacentini, the Italian architect who had come to collaborate in the University project, [12] Capanema had the winners receive the prizes that had been announced and then asked Lúcio Costa, one of those disqualified, to submit a new project. The young master insisted that the rest of the disqualified architects be asked too. With Lúcio Costa at the head, a group was formed consisting of Carlos Leão, Jorge Moreira and Affonso Eduardo Reidy, who were soon joined by Oscar Niemeyer and Ernani Vasconcellos. The new project for the Ministry of Education and Health was submitted in May, 1936. In June, Lúcio Costa suggested that Le Corbusier be invited to give his opinion on it, as well as on the project for University City. The invitation was transmitted by an old acquaintance, Alberto Monteiro de Carvalho. Le Corbusier accepted it, came to Rio, and for nearly one month lived in close association with the group of young architects, studying the suggested alternatives. At the outset he disapproved of the chosen location, on the Castelo Esplanade, in the new business section, and suggested another, for which he made a sketch, on the waterfront in the neighborhood of the present Santos Dumont Airport. Later he made another sketch for the site he had first rejected. He also drew, in a few days, a splendid preliminary suggestion for the University City, on a location later abandoned. At the same time that he was teaching and inspiring his immediate group of collaborators, Le Corbusier was reaching a wider audience through six lectures which he gave during the first two weeks of August. The new works of European architecture that Alberto Monteiro de Carvalho, A. Szilard and others had been patiently trying to expound to their colleagues who had not been out of the country, suddenly, with the words of

5

Le Corbusier, took on body and soul. His stay in Rio de Janeiro was thus of immeasurable instructive value and an unforgettable and lasting influence.

After he left, the Brazilian group went on with their work and in January, 1937, they submitted their final plan, a variation of Le Corbusier's. It showed the effects of their productive association with him as well as their own great talents and capacity for intelligent assimilation. In the finished building, a landmark of contemporary architecture, an incomparable degree of excellence was attained at one bound. The Ministry of Education and Health remains a high point in modern architecture, not only in Brazil but in the western world, a definitive contribution to the artistic heritage of our time.

Lúcio Costa resigned in 1939, without ceasing to act as advisor to the group. On the occasion of his resignation the other members elected Oscar Niemeyer to succeed to his duties. Niemeyer's extraordinary career, more than fulfilling his early promise, dates from this point. In his imaginative and highly personal work the modern international style undergoes a transmutation into a style deeply and instinctively appropriate to the Brazilian scene. His growing influence is shown predominantly in the work of most of the younger men, and he is internationally known as is no other Brazilian architect. In 1947 he was a member of the group that planned the United Nations Headquarters in New York, and his plan, with that of Le Corbusier, formed the point of departure for the final one. In 1955 he was asked to collaborate in the planning of a new quarter in Berlin, the Hansa district, where the 1958 International Architectural Exhibition will be held, for which he designed an apartment building, as did Van der Rohe, Gropius, Le Corbusier and Aalto. Also in 1955 he drew up a project for the new Museum of Modern Art in Caracas, Venezuela.

In February 1937, the year construction was begun on the Ministry of Education and Health, Attílio Corrêa Lima won the compe-

An azulejo façade, Alcantara, Maranhão, early xixth century

tition for the Seaplane Station in Rio de Janeiro (page 224). Although they could not refrain from calling attention to the poor quality of the rendering of the winning design, the jury had the perceptiveness to award him first prize, a decision fully justified by the merit and beauty of the completed building. A pioneer of the new architecture and a progressive city-planner, Attílio Corrêa Lima was, unfortunately, not to live to carry on his work. He died on August 27, 1943 in an aviation disaster near his Seaplane Station in which Brazil suffered the loss of several of her most distinguished writers and scientists. Milton Roberto was another pioneer, both daring and competent, who died some years later, while still young, the victim of a heart attack while presiding at an assembly of the Institute of Architects of Brazil, on July 15, 1953. In June, 1936, Marcelo and Milton Roberto won the competition

for the Brazilian Press Association building (the ABI), the first building in which the possibilities of the fixed *brise-soleil* were realized (see page 194). Niemeyer's Day Nursery, finished in 1937, was later to become the first example of the movable *brise-soleil* integrated with the architecture (see page 144).

The choice of architects for public buildings was more frequently made by means of competitions, according to the rules set up by the Institute of Architects of Brazil, and the more important projects were distinguished by a series of good selections. The competition for the Brazilian Pavilion at the New York World's Fair was won by Lúcio Costa in 1938; he, however, feeling that Oscar Niemeyer's plan was exceptionally interesting, invited him to join him in the working out of the final project, an unparalleled example of professional conscientiousness. In New York they evolved a new project together. The Brazilian Pavilion, completed in 1939, was one of the most popular attractions of the Fair and was generally

Grandjean de Montigny, Imperial Academy of Fine Arts, Rio de Janeiro, 1826 (subsequently used for the Finance Ministry; top floor was added later)

L. L. Vauthier, Santa Isabel Theater, Recife, Pernambuco, about 1845

regarded as its finest example of modern achitecture. The two Roberto brothers had won the competition for the Santos Dumont Airport at Calabouço Point in Rio de Janeiro in 1937. Henrique E. Mindlin, in 1942, won the competition for the new addition to the Ministry of Foreign Affairs (the Itamaraty Palace), and Affonso Eduardo Reidy and Jorge Moreira were jointly awarded first place in the competition for the central office building of the Rio Grande do Sul Railway, in Porto Alegre, in 1944.

In 1942, Philip L. Goodwin, who with Edward Stone had designed the Museum of Modern Art in New York, came to Brazil, like a new explorer, in order to put together an exhibition of Brazilian architecture. He was accompanied by G. E. Kidder Smith, now world-famous as a photographer of architecture. The exhibition that Goodwin organized at the Museum of Modern Art in New

York in 1943, and his fascinating book, the first of its kind, 'Brazil Builds', revealed a new work, full of charm and novelty, the first large-scale application of the principles of Le Corbusier, Gropius and Van der Rohe, an architecture which in other parts of the world had materialized earlier, in the first phase of International Architecture, but which in Brazil had now found artistic expression. There was immediate and dramatic foreign recognition, and Brazil awoke to the fact that her modern architecture was one of her most worthwhile contributions to contemporary culture. The man in the street, skeptical and ironical by nature, began to take pride in the buildings that at first he had considered funny or outlandish. He continued to give them nicknames, the privilege of the sidewalk critic, but underneath them one feels admiration and respect, and these buildings have become a part of his deep-seated pride in and affection for his city.

More and more visitors came from other countries, students, and architects young and old, curious to see for themselves the work of their Brazilian counterparts. Like Frank Lloyd Wright fifteen years before (when he supported the students on strike in Rio), Richard Neutra aroused the enthusiasm of the younger generation by lectures in which he earnestly discussed the human and social aspects of architecture. Paul Lester Wiener and Jose Luis Sert came to design Motor City for the government owned *Fabrica Nacional de Motores*, and Sert revived interest in the work of the International Congresses of Modern Architecture (CIAM). More recently the Biennial Exhibitions in São Paulo, in 1951, 1953, and 1955, have brought together, along with huge international displays of the plastic arts, exhibitions of modern architecture and of students' designs. Siegfried Giedion, Junzo Sakakura, Mario Pani, on the jury of the first Biennial; Walter Gropius, Alvar Aalto, and Ernesto Rogers on that of the second (the third showed only students' work and was judged by a local jury), established new points of contact with the international movement. More and more articles about Brazilian work appeared in foreign reviews, or special issues were devoted to it.

To all appearances the modern movement had triumphed in Brazil. Unfortunately, appearances are deceptive. There still remains a tremendous amount to be done before the architect's proper activity, his function as an organizer of space, can be brought home to the mass of the population.

In the last fifteen years an appreciable amount of work of undisputed merit has grown up, exactingly carried out within the limitations set by an industrial production in its infancy. But this achievement is somewhat offset by the large number of doubtful productions, in which a misunderstanding of the basic principles of modern architecture is betrayed. This is an inevitable result of the fantastically high building rate inherent in Brazilian economic development and, if only by the law of averages, there is bound to be a certain number of inferior buildings, until enough

time has elapsed for a correct viewpoint to be accepted and for efficient building techniques to be more generally adopted. Still, even the poorer contemporary buildings indicate that imitators are trying to follow the right lines.

On the other hand, the madly accelerated growth of the cities and expansion of industry have created a crying need for city-planning. Actually, in spite of the detailed royal orders on the lay-out of new towns brought by the early Portuguese colonizers, there is no historical record of any real, long-range, city-planning in Brazil. Although, surprising as it may seem, the city of Recife had paved sidewalks before Paris [13], there was never, in colonial days or under the Empire, any consistent attempt at planning, nor any single example comparable in importance to the Renaissance or Baroque achievements in Europe. Only in our time, under pressure of the pernicious effects of the lack of planning, has the need been felt for regulating the streets, relieving the congestion of traffic by classi-

The neo-colonial reaction/Solar de Monjope, designed by the owner, José Marianno Filho, Rio de Janeiro, 1926

fying and organizing it, zoning laws, and the systematizing of the city so that it can serve modern life adequately and agreeably. This is slow and painful work, obviously hindered by the large number of conflicting interests which have to be reconciled. Besides this, the rapidity of growth of the larger cities and the urgency of their immediate problems are such that it is almost impossible to see any opportunity in the near future for the radical modifications demanded by a master plan. The new cities (Londrina, Marilia, etc.) have grown under pressure from short-sighted real estate interests and they are expanding at such a rate that they have not been able to do much more in the way of city-planning than the older ones.

School of Grandjean de Montigny, Building at 38 Praça Servulo Dourado / Rio de Janeiro, 1848

School of L. L. Vauthier, House at 36, Rua Rosa e Silva, Recife, Pernambuco, middle xixth *century*

Gregori Warchavchik, House at Rua Itápolis, Pacaembú, São Paulo, 1928

Gregori Warchavchik, House at Rua Thomé de Souza, São Paulo, 1929

Gregori Warchavchik, Detail of house for Antonio da Silva Prado Neto, São Paulo, 1931

Nevertheless, some cities have tried to develop systematic master plans. The first to submit one was São Paulo, whose city authorities published a 'Plan of Avenues for the City of São Paulo' by F. Prestes Maia in 1930. Towards the end of the same year the French city planner, Alfred Agache, who had been hired by Mayor Antônio Prado Jr. in 1927, submitted a plan for Rio de Janeiro whose chief virtue was to arouse the municipal administration's interest in an overall plan as opposed to the partial plans that had been considered up till then. Revoked in 1934 on the grounds that it would take fifty years to carry out, it was taken up again in 1938, with the setting up of the City Planning Commission (see page 230). At an early date, the razing of Castelo Hill to provide an open area for the expansion of the business district, offered an instance of courageous dealing with city-planning problems. The same may be said of the opening up of Avenida Presidente Vargas (see page 230) under a financial scheme in which the benefits of the increase in land values accrued directly to the city treasury, and not to a few fortunate property owners. In our day, one can point to the razing of Santo Antonio Hill (see page 232), and to the filling in of a long strip along the waterfront at Calabouço, Flamengo and Botafogo, to provide wider thoroughfares, new parking and landscaped areas (see page 230). Curiously enough, as far back as 1798 a Dr. Antônio Joaquim de Medeiros had already suggested that Castelo and Santo Antônio Hills be razed, 'only the convent being kept in its site'. [14] Here, perhaps, the plan for Belo Horizonte should be mentioned. This new capital of Minas Gerais, an artificial city, like Washington, was begun in 1898 and the plan was drawn up by Aarão Reis in 1903. A gridiron with a superimposed network of diagonals, it did not take the topography of the region into account, with the result that in many sections of the city there are streets with a slope of more than 20%.

Other architects and city planners connected with the master plans of various Brazilian cities should be mentioned: Attilio Corrêa Lima (Goiania, capital of the state of Goiás, and Niterói, capital of the state of Rio de Janeiro); Nestor de Figueiredo (Recife, capital of Pernambuco); Edvaldo Paiva, Demetrio Ribeiro and Edgard Graeff (Florianopolis, capital of Santa Catarina); the last group and Francisco Macêdo, Nelson Souza and Roberto Veronese (Caxias do Sul, Rio Grande do Sul); José de Oliveira Reis (Ribeirão Preto, São Paulo); Luiz Sáia (Lins, São Paulo); and Léo Ribeiro de Moraes, with many plans for new cities under development. In 1950 the city of São Paulo invited Mr. Robert Moses, Park Commissioner of New York City, to undertake the study of 'A Program of Public Improvements', sponsored by the International Basic Economy Corporation. More recently, the scheme written into the Federal Constitution as early as 1891, for transporting the capital of the Republic to the interior of the country has again come before the public eye. A special commission, under the direction of Marshal José Pessoa, has decided on the location of the future capital—in the Central Highlands, state of Goiás, about six hundred miles northwest of Rio de Janeiro—and begun the study of the actual plan.

Still another problem of the greatest importance for the future development of modern architecture must be mentioned: the problem of teaching it. Formerly combined with the teaching of the fine arts or of engineering, it became independent of them in 1945 with the creation of separate Schools of Architecture in the various universities in the country. As the principal means of training young architects, work in established architectural offices, in direct contact with the day-to-day problems of professional practice, was substituted for the old atelier system inherited from

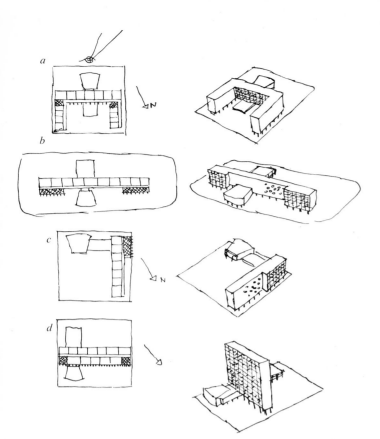

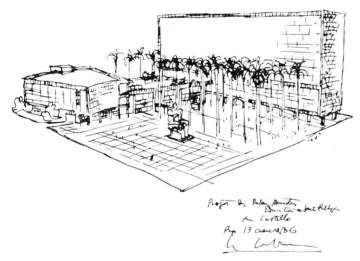

The evolution of the design for the Ministry of Education and Health, Rio de Janeiro, 1936–37. a *Brazilian group of architects*. b *Le Corbusier's scheme for the site near the airport*. c *Le Corbusier's scheme for the present site*. d *Final scheme by the Brazilian group*.

Le Corbusier, *Sketch for the Ministry of Education and Health, on the present site, Rio de Janeiro, 1936*

the École des Beaux Arts. Yet up till now little has been done to bring the curriculum up to date or give life to teaching methods. Attempts to apply the theories of the Bauhaus, either in their original form or with modifications suggested by North American experience, are still confined to an isolated case or two. Actually — not because there are not good teachers, but because, for practical purposes, the curriculum is still unintegrated, especially with regard to creative and artistic aspects — the architectural student of today remains, and will remain until the situation improves, exactly like his colleagues who created the modern architecture of Brazil — self-taught.

In contrast, labor problems are being met more systematically and

Luiz Nunes and Fernando Saturnino de Brito, *Water tower, Olinda, Pernambuco, 1937*

realistically. Workmanship, naturally mostly Portuguese to begin with and later refined, during the nineteenth century, especially in the south, by an influx of Italian and German immigrants, suffered badly from the transition after the first World War from a predominantly agricultural economy to one of increasing industrialization, made necessary by the import difficulties caused by the war. This transition also made it necessary to adjust to new methods of construction and industrial technique, and at first this had to be painfully re-done for each new job. At present, however, a promising beginning of standardized training has been made by the hundred and seven schools of the National Industrial Apprenticeship Service (SENAI), scattered throughout the country, with over 30 000 students (see page 140). Also, the possibilities and resources of industry itself are growing by leaps and bounds, reducing the actual building problems of the architect from day to day. Formerly, almost all tools, equipment and finishing materials had to be impor-

Rino Levi, *Interior of the Art Palacio movie theater, São Paulo, 1936*

Rino Levi, Interior of the Ipiranga movie theater, São Paulo, 1944

ted; now a greater of part them are being made in the country. The movement to standardize them has gradually grown with the improvement of manufacturing methods and products. The Brazilian Technical Norms Association was set up in 1940 and in a few years has had to codify an enormous body of specifications and standards; it is already paving the way for the use of modular coordination. Finally, some of the circumstances that hinder the development of modern architecture in Brazil should be taken into consideration. Brazil is often described as being 'as big as the United States—i.e. the United States of North America—, plus a second state of Texas. Its approximately 60 000 000 inhabitants (1956) are a relatively sparse population for its 3 386 170 square miles (8 550 000 square kilometers). One major hindrance is the lack of adequate transportation; another is the shortage of capital. Although the railroads stand 9th in the world in total mileage, they rank 71st in mileage rate per square mile of territory, and 47th in mileage

Night view of Rio de Janeiro

View of Rio de Janeiro from Corcovado

rate per capita. Until very recently Brazil's road transportation system depended entirely on imported oil and gasoline; only now are refineries being set up and the country's own oil supplies being tapped. And although the civil aviation system is the second largest in the world, it cannot at present serve the transportation needs of the construction industry. Finally, the lack of capital from which the country has suffered since the first World War is reflected in the current extremely high rates of interest and in the handicap they create for long term investment. This has its effect on any building program and makes it difficult to formulate any permanent policy either in public or private building.

Before examining further the characteristics of present-day Brazilian architecture, two factors that have contributed decisively to its formation should be singled out. The first of these has been research into the functions of sunlight. In São Paulo, where the problem very often is to get all the sunlight possible rather than, as in Rio de Janeiro, to avoid it, Alexandre Albuquerque, the beloved teacher of so many architects, published the first relevant scientific study of the subject in 1916. Developing earlier studies of Lucio Martins Rodrigues at the Polytechnic School of São Paulo, he established a scientific basis for the orientation and sunlighting of buildings. As a result of his work, the building code of São Paulo was the first in the world to put into effect the recommendations of the First International Congress for the Sanitation of the Dwelling, held in Paris, 1904, and to set up mathematical rules for obtaining the required amount of sunlight in all buildings. For example, according to this code, on the day of the winter solstice, June 21 (near St. John's day, one of the most popular Brazilian holidays,) which on this side of the equator is the shortest day in the year, the rays of the sun must touch, in every building in the city, no matter

View of the central district of São Paulo

View of Avenida Presidente Vargas, with Candelaria Church in the foreground, Rio de Janeiro

Lúcio Costa, Detail of Bristol apartment building, Rio de Janeiro, 1950

how briefly, the bottom of any courtyard or lightwell that serves to light a living or dining room; in a bedroom, this must occur for at least one hour, between 11 A M and 1 P M, in the older sections of the city, and for three hours, between 9 A M and 3 P M, in the newer sections. Later, in Rio de Janeiro, Paulo Sá, Attilio Corrêa Lima, Hermínio de Andrade e Silva, and others went on independently with similar studies. Under the leadership of Paulo Sá, a body of doctrine was formulated, based on thorough experimental research, covering all aspects of the sunlight problem in buildings, astronomical as well as those of heat, glare, shade, and so on.

The second factor is the development of an advanced technique for the use of reinforced concrete, resulting not only in light and elegant structures but in appreciable economy in comparison with building costs in other countries[15]. A brilliant group of structural designers has kept pace with and assisted the work of the architects from the beginning: Emílio Baumgart, known as 'the father of reinforced concrete in Brazil' (Blumenau, Santa Catarina, 1889—Rio de Janeiro, 1943), Joaquim Cardoso, Antonio Alves de Noronha, Paulo Fragoso, W. Tietz, and many others. These two factors correspond directly to the two most conspicuous features of modern architecture in Brazil: the use of large surfaces of glass, protected when necessary by the *brise-soleil*, and the use of the free structure, standing on *pilotis*, with the ground floor open when possible. And both of these features show the marked influence of Le Corbusier.

The *brise-soleil* (in Portuguese *quebra-sol* or 'sun-breaker', but the French expression commonly used indicates its direct derivation, again, from Le Corbusier) has been applied in Brazil in the greatest variety of ways. Easily handled sunlight graphs and tables, in general use by architects for several decades now, make it possible to calculate accurately and to solve any sunlight problem. Movable

or fixed *brise-soleil*, vertical or horizontal, are designed according to the orientation of the building and its purposes in a great range of materials: reinforced concrete, aluminum, asbestos cement, sheet metal, glass wool inserted between glass sheets, in plywood sections or shutters set in sashes (aluminum *brise-soleil* are now being mass produced in São Paulo).

And while, in one way, any type of *brise-soleil* can be thought of as an imitation of the old traditional methods of protection against glare and heat, nevertheless the *brise-soleil* has undoubtedly added a new element to our architecture, both by its independence from the millwork in general and by its plastic integration with the façade, to which it gives even when fixed, but more especially when movable, a characteristic dynamic. If, as Le Corbusier says, architecture is 'the skilled, correct, and magnificent play of volumes under the light', the *brise-soleil* gives to the play and the volumes infinite richness of modulation, in a sense a fourth dimension, through the constant shifting of shadows across the surface from sunrise to sunset.

Reminiscences of and variations on the traditional colonial screens and shutters are frequently found in the details of the *brise-soleil*, as well as of the millwork, expressions from the past re-occurring in the vernacular now being formed, or new answers provided to the everpresent problems of tropical or sub-tropical climates. For example, open-work panels of hollow tiles or pre-cast concrete, severe or fanciful, soften the glare or cast lace-like patterns of shadow. Many varieties of trellises and jalousies—sometimes revivals of old designs, like the *muxarabis* (see page 22), or balustrades, are used almost in their original form, or occasionally on a magnified scale for more obvious and emphatic architectural accent. The free structure, or when that is not the natural solution, the structure honestly and clearly integrated with the design, is another

Lucjan Korngold, C B I building, São Paulo, 1949

facing. The generally hot and humid climate, with heavy rainfall (forty-seven inches a year in Rio) makes less resistant facings, such as stucco, impractical. Le Corbusier did us still another service when he suggested that the *azulejos* should be revived. Not only blue and white, as most frequently in the past, but in all colors and shades, the *azulejos* serve marvelously to accent the non-supporting character of vertical surfaces. In repeated patterns based on one or a certain number of pieces, usually four, or in large compositions, representational or abstract, panels of *azulejos* introduce a lively note of regionalism. With their new variations, panels of glass or porcelain mosaic, they constitute a link between painters and architects. Portinari, Burle Marx, Di Cavalcanti, Clóvis Graciano, Paulo Werneck (the first to use porcelain mosaic), Anisio Medeiros and Wilson Reis Neto have all designed interesting panels for important building projects. It is also true that such panels have been sadly overdone or put to trivial or vulgar uses; but the recent develop-

Mass-produced aluminum brise-soleil, São Paulo, 1955

important characteristic. While not of special merit in itself, its most direct consequence is the increasingly common use of *pilotis* in the ground floor. Practicable in Brazil because of the climate, the freeing of the ground floor vindicates all the claims Le Corbusier has made for it and results in a better integration of interior and exterior space. In Rio de Janeiro a law has recently been passed to the effect that the ground floor, when of *pilotis*, is not counted in the number of floors allowed by the Building Code. Although passed too late to be of much value in the older districts, where many new buildings with open ground floors must be placed between others solid to the ground, this law encourages more open planning in the newer districts (besides contributing to better organized structural design, since the structural scheme becomes visible at street level). Undoubtedly the concept of *pilotis* should, ideally, be related to more modern concepts of city-planning and a freer use of the land than prevail at present. In Rio de Janeiro, cut up as it is into small-sized lots, perhaps it might have represented the final victory of the street over the private house (in this case apartment house) in the struggle begun in Bahia two hundred years ago. From the few examples already in existence, one can imagine how much more comfortable and attractive Copacabana would have been if the apartment houses, now lined up along streets parallel to the beach and presenting a solid barrier to any ventilation whatever, had all been raised on *pilotis* and could let the sea breezes blow through the entire district freely, up to the mountains rising behind them.

Another way in which the colonial tradition has been appropriately adapted to present necessity is in the use of *azulejos* as wall

Henrique E. Mindlin, House for Romeu S. Mindlin, São Paulo, 1946

Affonso Eduardo Reidy, House for Dr. O. B. Couto e Silva, Estrada da Tijuca, Rio de Janeiro, 1955

ment of abstract and concrete painting in Brazil will probably encourage their better use.

Opportunities offered to the sculptor have been lamentably less. Even if a few works by artists like Alfredo Ceschiatti, Mario Cravo, Bruno Giorgi, Maria Martins, José Pedrosa, and Auguste Zamoiski (not to mention Lipchitz's 'Prometheus Unbound' for the Ministry of Education and Health) have been incorporated into some building projects, it is undeniable that the sculptor has not been able to participate in the architectural movement of his day to anything like the degree he did in the eighteenth century.

In the applied arts the contemporary spirit is more and more in evidence. In the furniture of Joaquim Tenreiro and others the rebirth of fine craftsmanship is preparing the way for the future manufacturing of good modern furniture. In fabrics for interior decoration Fayga Ostrower, a well-known engraver, has succeeded in giving a regional character to fine abstract designs. The same is true of the hand-woven fabrics and rugs made by Lili Correia de Araujo, Regina Graz, Madeleine Collaço, and Genaro Carvalho, and of the ceramics of Elizabeth Nobiling, Margaret Spence and Carlo Hauner. It is in the sphere of gardens, however, that this regional character shows the greatest vitality. Since the early gardens [16] of Roberto Burle Marx (1934) and Attilio Corrêa Lima (1938), modern architecture finds appropriate and harmonious setting in the work of specialists like David Azambuja, Carlos Perry, Roberto Cardoso Coelho, Suzana Osborn, and others. And in the work of Roberto Burle Marx contemporary landscape gardening reaches a level on which it plays a role equivalent in its field to that of contemporary architecture itself.

The poetic imagination of Burle Marx (who is also a distinguished painter and fabric designer) has, combined with his wide knowledge of tropical flora and his constant search for hitherto neglected plants from the depths of the interior for introduction into the gardens, created a true school of Brazilian landscape architecture. In the inventiveness and plastic luxuriance of these gardens Brazilian architecture finds its natural habitat. In Burle Marx's more recent work the composition has been increasingly disciplined and expresses the artist's growing maturity economically and directly.

The parallel between the achievement of Burle Marx and that of modern Brazilian architecture is so close that, with due allowance for the difference in scope and scale, they can almost be described in the same terms: emotional spontaneity, striving for integration with the circumstances of land and climate, and re-assessment of the plastic language and of the means of expression, all under a growing intellectual discipline.

The following pages illustrate, within the possibilities of this book, some of the more significant work from the beginning of the movement until the present day. In them the reader may perhaps discover for himself cause for more specific appreciation.

The pictures on pages 15–19 illustrate projects of historical interest or noteworthy uncompleted jobs which could not fit into the general plan of presentation adopted throughout the book.

NOTES

[1] *Lúcio Costa, 'Arquitetura Brasileira', col. 'Os Cadernos de Cultura', Serviço de Documentação, Ministério da Educação e Saúde, Rio de Janeiro, 1952, page 41.*
[2] *Gilberto Freyre, 'Sobrados e Mucambos', Livraria José Olympio Editora, Rio de Janeiro, 1951, 2nd Edition, Volume 2, page 395.*
[3] *Livro de Posturas do Senado da Camara da Cidade do Salvador, 2. fl. 4, 1696 (Robert Smith, 'Documentos Baianos', 'Revista do Serviço do Patrimônio Histórico e Artístico Nacional', nº 9, Minis-*

View of Avenida Atlantica, Copacabana, Rio de Janeiro

Mosaic designed by E. Di Cavalcanti for the Cultura Artistica Theater (Rino Levi and Roberto Cerqueira Cesar, architects), São Paulo, 1949

tério da Educação e Saúde, Rio de Janeiro, 1945, page 94). Later, in 1785, even the proportions of the stories, doors, windows and balconies are laid down in detailed regulations.

[4] *José Wasth Rodrigues, 'A Casa de Moradia no Brasil Antigo', in 'Revista do* SPHAN', *nº 9, Ministério da Educação e Saúde, Rio de Janeiro, 1945, page 160.*

[5] *Robert Smith, loc. cit. As Chief Justice João Rodrigues de Brito said of the window-screens in Bahia, at the beginning of the eighteenth century: 'The jalousies also obstruct civilization, hiding the fair sex from the male one, only for it to peep out on the sly and always shame-faced. The destruction of this Moorish hiding-place would put the ladies in the position of having to clothe themselves better to come to the windows to satisfy the natural curiosity of seeing and being seen, and thus familiarizing themselves with the male sex, they would not make a virtue of the unsocial reclusion, which causes them to shun men, as though they were excommunicates'. Idem, page 99.*

[6] *'Architecture Toscane ou Palais, Maisons et autres édifices de la Toscane, mesurés et dessinés, par A. Grandjean de Montigny et A. Famin, Architectes, anciens pensionnaires de l'Académie de France, à Rome', Didot, Paris, 1815, subsequently republished in New York, 1932, with the same title, by The Pencil Points Press.*

[7] *Gilberto Freyre, in the introduction to 'Casas de Residência no Brasil' by L. L. Vauthier, 'Revista do* SPHAN' *nº 7, Rio de Janeiro, 1943, page 109.*

[8] *A reaction which also occurred in other countries of America, springing from generalized nativistic and regionalistic impulses, possibly related to the Monroe Doctrine ('America for the Americans'). On a more strictly architectural plane, an interesting parallel may be drawn with European movements such as, in England, the return of Norman Shaw to the Queen Anne style in 1890. Its most positive significance, magnificently expressed by Gilberto Freyre in the Regionalist Manifesto (Recife, 1926), was only later to take definite shape in architecture with the more recent attempts at integrating contemporary elements with regional and traditional ones.*

[9] *The Modern Art Week was held in February, 1922, and comprised three festivals organized by Graça Aranha (1868–1931), Mario de Andrade (1893–1945), Paulo Prado (1869–1943) and Ronald de Carvalho (1893–1935), on the 11th, 15th and 17th, and devoted to: painting and sculpture; literature and poetry; philosophy and modern criticism; music. Amongst others and in addition to those already mentioned, the following personalities took part: Villa-Lobos, Oswald de Andrade (1890–1954), Manuel Bandeira, Renato de Almeida, Alvaro Moreyra, Ribeiro Couto, Rubens Borba de Moraes, Menotti del Picchia Sérgio Milliet, Afonso Schmidt, Guiomar Novaes, René Thiollier, Guilherme de Almeida and Cândido Motta Filho. The artists who exhibited their works for eight days in the foyer of the Municipal Theater included: Vitor Brecheret (1894–1955), sculptor; Anita Malfati, Di Cavalcanti (one of the first to support the movement), Oswaldo Goeldi, Regina Graz, J. F. de Almeida Prado, painters; and A. Moya and J. Przyrembel, archi-*

Sergio W. Bernardes, Exhibition Pavilion for Companhia Siderurgica Nacional, Ibirapuéra Park, São Paulo, 1954

tects. In the 'anthropophagist' movement of 1928, the name of Raul Bopp, its leader, must be singled out.

[10] *'Il Piccolo', an Italian newspaper published in São Paulo, June 14, 1925, and 'Correio da Manhã', Rio de Janeiro, November 1, 1925.*

[11] *In a reception at the São Paulo City Hall on November 23, 1929, Le Corbusier was acclaimed by Mr. Goffredo da Silva Telles as 'one of the most outstanding figures in French intellectual circles'. After delivering a short address, Le Corbusier had to leave before the end of the session in order to make an 'excursion by plane over the city'. 'Correio Paulistano', São Paulo, November 24, 1929, page 12.*

[12] *Mario de Andrade (1893–1945), a great writer and critic of music and the fine arts, was the leading figure in the modern movement in São Paulo; Carlos Drummond de Andrade and Manuel Bandeira are two of the foremost contemporary Brazilian poets; Rodrigo Mello Franco de Andrade, as head of the Serviço do Patrimônio Histórico e Artístico Nacional (*SPHAN*), the federal department for the preservation and restoration of historical and artistic monuments, is responsible for invaluable achievement in the study and protection of our artistic heritage.*

[13] *L. L. Vauthier, Casas de Residência no Brasil, a series of letters to Cesar Daly, in the Revista do* SPHAN, *nº 7, Rio de Janeiro, 1943, page 177.*

[14] *Adolfo Morales de los Rios Filho, 'Grandjean de Montigny e a Evolução da Arte Brasileira', Empresa A Noite, Rio de Janeiro, undated, page 47.*

[15] *Steel had been used earlier in the century and Belem do Pará even boasts of a water tower designed by Gustave Eiffel. With the outbreak of the first World War, it became increasingly difficult and costly to import this material and its place was rapidly taken by reinforced concrete. Nowadays, with the development of the local steel industry, it is once more practical to explore the possibilities of metallic structures.*

[16] *The first garden landscaped by Roberto Burle Marx dates from 1934 and belongs to the Schwartz residence, designed by Lúcio Costa and Gregori Warchavchik, who were partners at the time. After that, he worked in Recife in 1935, '36 and '37 (see page 239). Attilio Corrêa Lima was already planning the garden of the Seaplane Station (page 224) in a regional manner in 1938.*

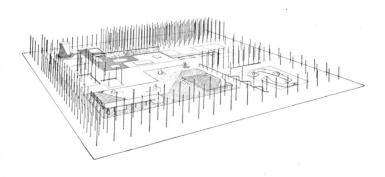

Roberto Burle Marx, Perspective sketch, plan for the Independence Plaza, João Pessoa, Paraíba, 1953

Oscar Niemeyer | Competition design for the National Stadium | 1941 | Rio de Janeiro

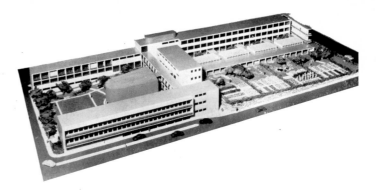

Giancarlo Palanti and Daniele Calabi | Children's Home for the League of Catholic Women | 1949 | São Paulo

Henrique E. Mindlin | Winning competition design for the new addition to the Ministry of Foreign Relations | 1942 | Rio de Janeiro

Rino Levi, F. A. Pestalozzi and Roberto Cerqueira Cesar | Maternity Hospital, University of São Paulo | 1946 | São Paulo (under construction)

Icaro de Castro Mello | Winning competition for the Esporte Club Sírio | 1950 | São Paulo (under construction)

Carlos Frederico Ferreira | Winning competition design for a covered swimming pool for Sociedade Esportiva Palmeiras | 1951 | São Paulo (under construction)

Henrique E. Mindlin | Project for a hotel at Praia Vermelha | 1946 | Rio de Janeiro

David Xavier Azambuja | State Government Palace | 1952 | Curitiba, Paraná

Ary Garcia Roza with Almir Gadelha, Aldo Garcia Roza and Waldyr Leal da Costa | Winning competition design for the new Bank of Brazil head-quarters | 1951 | Rio de Janeiro

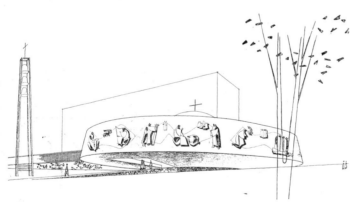

Sergio W. Bernardes | Winning competition design for the St. Dominic Chapel | 1952 | São Paulo

Eduardo Kneese de Mello | 'Japurá' apartment building | 1952 | São Paulo (under completion)

David Xavier Azambuja, Olavo Redig de Campos, F. A. Regis and Sergio Santos Rodrigues | Civic Center | 1952 | Curitiba, Paraná (under construction). In the background, right, the Government Palace, left, the Palace of Justice; in the foreground, right, the Legislative Assembly, left, Government departments building.

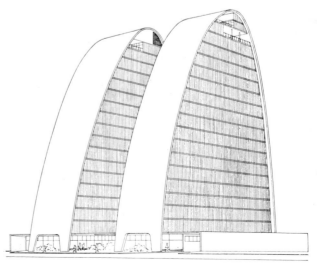

Rino Levi and Roberto Cerqueira Cesar | Design for two buildings for the 'São Paulo' National Life Insurance Company | 1952 | São Paulo

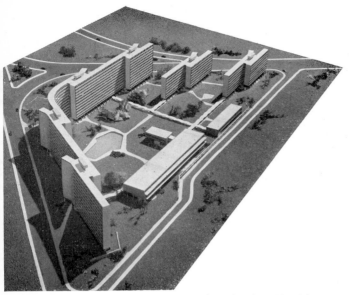

Affonso Eduardo Reidy | Brasil-Paraguay Experimental School | 1953 | Assunción, Paraguay (under construction)

Rino Levi and Roberto Cerqueira Cesar | Students' residential sector (University of São Paulo) | 1953 | São Paulo

José de Souza Reis and Alcides Rocha Miranda | University of São Paulo. Institute for the Primary School Teacher | 1953 | São Paulo (under construction)

Henrique E. Mindlin (Holabird & Root & Burgee, associate architects) | Design for Hotel Copan, Intercontinental Hotels Corporation | 1953 | São Paulo
Oscar Niemeyer | S-shaped Copan apartment building | 1953 | São Paulo (under construction)

Marcos Konder Neto | Motor boats racing observation post | 1954 | Rio de Janeiro

Oscar Niemeyer | 'Conjunto Governador Kubitschek' group | 1953–1954 | Belo Horizonte, Minas Gerais (under construction)

Flavio Marinho Rego | Deodoro Housing Development for the Fundação da Casa Popular (National Housing Foundation) | 1954 | Rio de Janeiro (under construction)

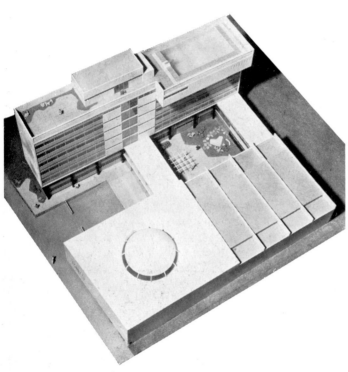

Oscar Niemeyer | State School of Belo Horizonte | 1954 | Belo Horizonte, Minas Gerais (under construction)

Henrique E. Mindlin | Winning competition design for a synagogue and community center for the Congregação Israelita Paulista | 1954 | São Paulo (under construction)

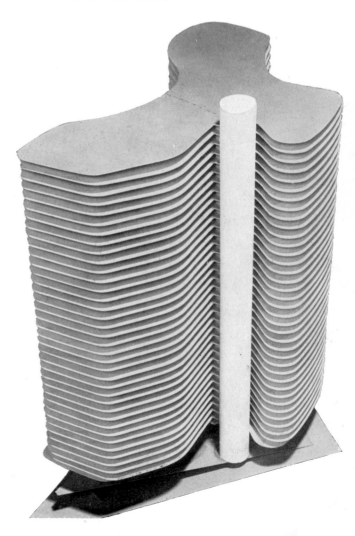

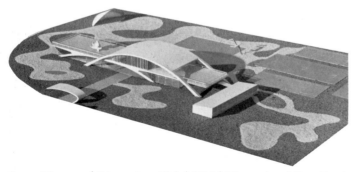

Oscar Niemeyer | Diamantina Club | 1954 | Diamantina, Minas Gerais (under construction)

Oscar Niemeyer | Twelve-story apartment building | 1954 | Belo Horizonte, Minas Gerais (under construction)

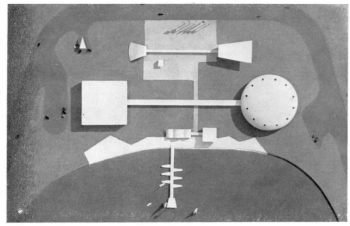

Oscar Niemeyer | TV and Radio Station for TV-Rio | 1954 | Rio de Janeiro

Paulo Antunes Ribeiro | Project for the Anchieta Residential Development for Banco Hipotecário Lar Brasileiro | 1955 | Rio de Janeiro

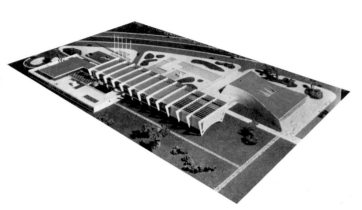

Affonso Eduardo Reidy | Museum of Modern Art of Rio de Janeiro | 1954 Rio de Janeiro (under construction)

David Libeskind | Design for the Conjunto Nacional, a hotel, apartments and shopping center development | 1955 | São Paulo (under construction)

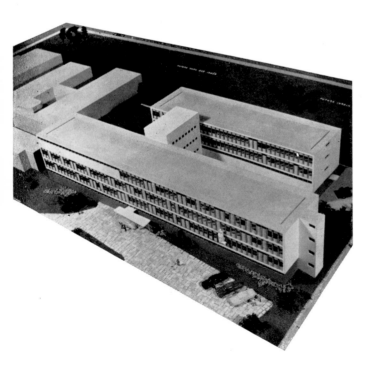

Oscar Niemeyer | Design for the Museum of Modern Art building | 1955 | Caracas, Venezuela

Jorge Wilheim | General Hospital (Santa Casa) | 1954 | Jaú, São Paulo (under construction)

Abelardo de Souza | Design for the Braz district Market Hall | 1955 | São Paulo (under construction)

Private Houses

Apartment Buildings, Hotels

Housing Projects

LÚCIO COSTA

House for Argemiro Hungria Machado / 1942 / Rio de Janeiro

This house illustrates an aspect of Lúcio Costa's manner related to his work for SPHAN (*Serviço do Patrimônio Histórico e Artístico Nacional*), devoted to careful restoration and reconstruction of the country's artistic and historical monuments. In it, traditional elements are worked into a discreetly expressed contemporary design. The massive construction, wide eaves, and colonial tiles; the symmetrical and tranquil fenestration of the main façade, the *muxarabis* of the patio—a nostalgic evocation of the past—all blend naturally with the more modern features of the project: outdoors brought into the interior by means of a veranda entirely open to the patio, the large door of movable wooden *brise-soleil* opening into the garden in front, and the sleeping porches adjoining each bedroom on the second story.

Standing on a corner lot, the house is built around a patio in order to give its owners the necessary privacy and to compensate for the comparative smallness of the land in proportion to the building. The dimensions of residential lots, almost always smaller than they should be for luxurious houses as well as more economical ones, are a constant problem in Brazilian cities and the inevitable result is extremely high real estate values.

Ground floor 1:400

Upper floor 1:400

1 Living
2 Patio
3 'Impluvium'
4 Veranda
5 Dining
6 Kitchen-Pantry
7 Food storage
8 Garage
9 Laundry and service yard
10 Maid
11 Bedroom
12 Sleeping porch
13 Study
14 Linen
15 Terrace
16 Upper part of patio

View of a 'muxarabi'

GREGORI WARCHAVCHIK

Seaside house for Count Raul Crespi / 1943 / Guarujá, São Paulo

The scarcity of land mentioned before was also a problem in this vacation and weekend house, built between the street and the beach at a seaside resort near Santos, the port of São Paulo. The architect, one of the pioneers of the modern movement in Brazil, made up for this defect by confining the garden to one side of the house and extending it through the covered terrace outside the living room. From this terrace, which, with the living room, forms an area of *pilotis* supporting the bedrooms, a suspended staircase that can be drawn up when not needed leads dripping bathers directly to the upper floor without their having to make use of the main staircase in the hall. All the bedrooms face the sea. The bathrooms are lighted by a clerestory above the bedroom corridor. The size and number of work areas and servants' rooms, around a small inside patio, show how comparatively easy it still is to get domestic help in Brazil.

The roof is of corrugated asbestos cement and the rolling shutters, of wood, are painted in bright-colored stripes reminiscent of beach tents and umbrellas.

1 Living
2 Dining
3 Bar
4 Kitchen-Pantry
5 Laundry
6 Service yard
7 Maid
8 Storage
9 Bedroom

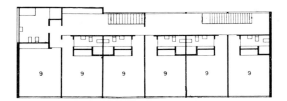

Upper floor 1:400   *Ground floor 1:400*

RINO LEVI

House for Rino Levi / 1946 / São Paulo

In this project for the architect's own house, the plan is the result of the irregular form and dimensions of the corner lot as well as of its unfavorable orientation. Because in São Paulo's climate as much sunlight as possible is a necessity, the living room faces a patio that receives it all day, and the master and servants' bedrooms have patios that receive afternoon sun. The setback required by city law is landscaped flush with the sidewalk without the customary fence or wall. The enclosed gardens were designed by Roberto Burle Marx and the views they provide, protected from the street and neighbors, make up a great deal for the flatness and monotony of the surrounding landscape.

All rooms have controlled cross ventilation. The bathrooms and dressing rooms are lighted by a clerestory above the bedroom corridor. The windows of the living and dining rooms open onto large roofless planted boxes, sealed on the outer side against sun and prowlers by louvers of pre-cast concrete.

The living and dining area (100 square meters, or about 1075 square feet) is conceived as a continuous space in which the entrance hall is marked off by a storage wall 2.10 meters (about 6' 10¾") high, extending at one end over the fireplace, with a coat closet on the hall side, and a bar, bookcases, and writing desk on the living room side.

1 Living
2 Dining
3 Planted box
4 Porch
5 Bedroom
6 Study
7 Maid
8 Kitchen-Pantry
9 Garage
10 Storage

Plan 1:400

ALDARY HENRIQUES TOLEDO

House for José Pacheco de Medeiros Filho / 1946 / Cataguázes, Minas Gerais

This house, in the same town in Minas Gerais as the Maternity Hospital shown on page 146, makes the most of the slope of the land to achieve an orderly and discreet spatial arrangement which is, at the same time, full of movement and has a great deal of variety in its interior perspectives. The lower floor is on two levels joined by an open gallery extending to the terrace, which communicates with the garden by a ramp as well as directly, by a staircase. The treatment of the veranda, with its uninterrupted wooden balustrade running in front of the slender posts supporting the roof, against the background of shuttered doors, is a characteristic example of elements from the past used in a contemporary manner.

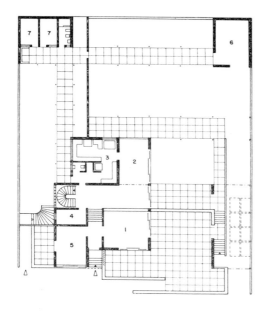

Ground floor 1:500

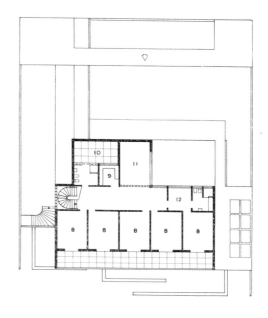

Upper floor 1:500

1 *Living*
2 *Dining*
3 *Kitchen-Pantry*
4 *Sewing room*
5 *Study*
6 *Garage*
7 *Maid*
8 *Bedroom*
9 *Linen*
10 *Sunporch*
11 *Upper part of Dining room*
12 *Dressing room*

GREGORI WARCHAVCHIK

Beach Pavilion for Mrs. Jorge Prado / 1946 / Guarujá, São Paulo

In contrast to the Aldary Toledo house, this little pavilion, which already plays a part in the social life of São Paulo, shows sophistication of a different kind, partly disguised by the extreme simplicity of its construction: ordinary brickwork, roofed with local thatch *(sapé)* and floored with round sections of tree trunks embedded in cement. The ceiling, the doors and the window shutters are of planks covered with straw matting and, for easier upkeep, no glass has been used anywhere.

At present the headquarters of the 'Jequiti-Mar' beach club, it is part of a project (shown on page 234) promoted by the owners for the improvement and development of the whole area, which is known as Pernambuco Beach.

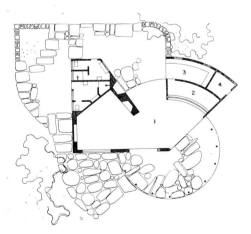

Plan 1:400

1 Living
2 Bar
3 Kitchen
4 Storage

ITALO EUGÊNIO MAURO

House for Italo Eugênio Mauro / 1947 / São Paulo

In this example of a particularly small and badly oriented lot, the designer, by means of a truly three-dimensional planning of the living areas, has not only succeeded in creating a dynamic interior quite unexpected from the street approach, but also managed to provide for as much sunlight as possible. The high-ceilinged living room (15′5″ or 4.70 meters), with its north wall entirely of glass, faces the rear of the lot. This also brings sun into the entrance area, used at different times as a bar or as a dining place for the children, as well as into the study on the mezzanine level. The vines on the two pergolas outside the glass wall of the living room help shut out the excessive summer sun and, leafless in winter, let its slanting beams enter when most needed.

The garage, a simple shelter, also serves as a passageway to the laundry area and service entrance.

A bedroom (indicated in the section) had to be added later over the highest part of the living room to provide for an increase in the family. The horizontal divisions in the glass wall are for protection against intruders.

Ground floor 1:400

Upper floor 1:400

1 Living
2 Dining
3 Kitchen-Pantry
4 Maid
5 Carport
6 Bedroom
7 Study

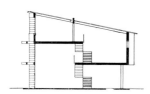

Section 1:400

CARLOS FREDERICO FERREIRA

Week-end house for Carlos Frederico Ferreira / 1949 / Friburgo Mountains, Rio de Janeiro

Built with even more rudimentary techniques than Mrs. Jorge Prado's beach pavilion (page 29), the entire cost of this charming house was then about equal to that of a Volkswagen automobile. The system adopted was that of *páu-a-pique* (literally stuck wood), rather like a wattle and adobe construction, still very common in the interior of Brazil, in which a framework of wood, including branches and twigs, is filled in with clay without the need of further binding.

The roof rests on the walls except in the living room, where it is supported on an independent structure of wooden poles, permitting greater freedom in the treatment of the façade. Originally of *sapé* (local thatch), the roof was later changed to terra-cotta half-round tiles.

The colors used on the walls combine whitewash with yellow, the traditional colonial blue, and the natural shades of the gray stone and wood (only impregnated with a colorless protective substance).

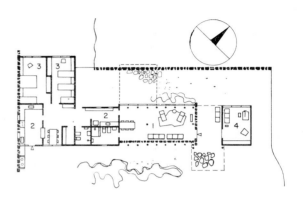

Section 1:400

1 *Living-Dining*
2 *Kitchen-Pantry*
3 *Bedroom*
4 *Study*

Plan 1:400

J. VILANOVA ARTIGAS
House for Heitor Almeida / 1949 / Santos, São Paulo

Originally influenced by Frank Lloyd Wright, Artigas has rapidly evolved a characteristic personal point of view, retaining only Wright's feeling of spatial continuity. In the house below, this feeling is accentuated not only by the patio integrated with the volume of the building as a whole, but by the ramp connecting the two blocks, which leads to the study on an intermediate level and, a little above the bedrooms, to the sunporch placed over the study and maid's room. The slight elevation of the ground floor and patio in relation to the street leaves room for the garage and laundry, on the level of the sidewalk in the lower part of the smaller block.

A band of *brise-soleil* stretches across the bedroom windows permitting the control of sunlight even when the shutters are open. These work on a counterbalance principle, the upper half rising when the lower half is lowered, and *vice versa*.

Artigas thinks of modern man as dominating and ordering his environment, in search of a suitable framework for an integrated and harmonious society. Therefore, instead of submission to the landscape, and a fusion with nature, he prefers a clear and honest expression of contemporary methods and techniques. If this occasionally seems rather dry and doctrinaire, it never ceases to show an undercurrent of consistent poetic feeling.

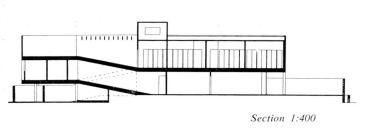

Section 1:400

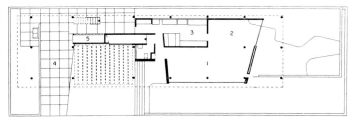

Ground floor 1:400

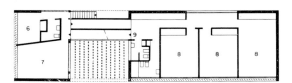

Upper floor 1:400

1 Living
2 Dining
3 Kitchen
4 Garage
5 Storage
6 Maid
7 Study
8 Bedroom
9 Ramp to sun porch

J. VILANOVA ARTIGAS

House for J. Vilanova Artigas / 1949 / São Paulo

In this extremely compact and economical residence, the architect's own, he states his feeling of spatial interpenetration even more clearly than in the preceding example.

The terrace adjoining the living-room and extending beneath the study connects the two, and at the same time it is open on three sides to a garden which occupies the greater part of the land. A single and continuous volume thus includes all the living area, separated from the exterior only by the wide walls, entirely glazed with the direct and simple detail that is so highly characteristic of Artigas.

Section 1:400

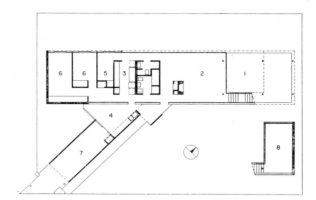

1 Terrace
2 Living-Dining
3 Kitchen
4 Service yard
5 Maid
6 Bedroom
7 Garage
8 Study

Plan 1:400

ENRIQUE E. MINDLIN

Country House for George Hime / 1949 / Bonclima, near Petrópolis, Rio de Janeiro

A three-dimensional, dynamic spatial organization is also found in this country house, which received the prize for the best private dwelling at the First Biennial in São Paulo, in 1951. The plan follows the slope of the land; the living area is divided into a large living room on the upper level, another on the lower, and a game room extending into the *pilotis* area. This last forms a large covered terrace, partly sheltered by a wind-break decorated with a highly colored mosaic mural by Roberto Burle Marx, who also laid out the garden. The dining room slab, suspended over the lower part of the living room, is at the eye level of anyone seated by the fireplace at the stone wall. A large mobile, especially made for this house by Alexander Calder, provides an effective focal point for the composition.

One of the ways in which the interior and exterior are linked is the retaining wall that extends into the garden. The differences in texture of the stone work used in this retaining wall and in the fireplace wall emphasize its use as a structural material in one case and as a facing material in the other.

The living room has the best view, while the bedrooms face north for maximum sun during the colder winter months. There is direct access from the carport, beneath the service wing, to both upper and lower levels of the house. In the bedrooms the windows and their shutters work on the counterbalance principle. In the lower halves of the shutters, hinged panels swing outwards to admit light when shutters are closed, permitting easy regulation of sun and light, as well as giving a personal touch to the façade.

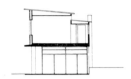

Section 1 1:400

1 Living
2 Dining
3 Bedroom
4 Cloak-room and W.C.
5 Kitchen-Pantry
6 Maid
7 Laundry
8 Storage
9 Covered terrace
10 Carport

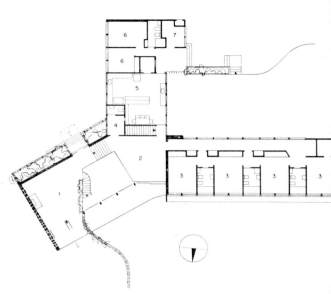

Upper floor 1:400

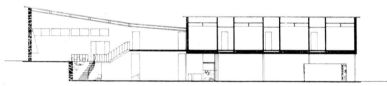

Section 2 1:400

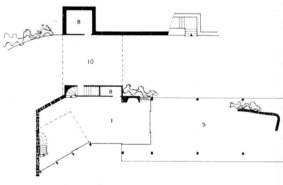

Lower floor 1:400

FRANCISCO BOLONHA

Country house for Ambassador Hildebrando Accioly / 1950 / Fazenda Inglêsa, near Petrópolis, Rio de Janeiro

This summer residence in the mountains little more than an hour's drive from Rio de Janeiro has been generously planned for a numerous family and their guests, and its integration in imposing and dramatic scenery has been deliberately sought. The materials, of local origin whenever possible, have been used with the greatest simplicity, and according to artisan tradition. The stone walls of the living room are left undressed both inside and out, and match the scale of the wide wooden planks of the floor.

All the rooms are planned in close connection with the exterior, and open either onto the garden, or onto planted patios. A covered gallery, entirely of wood, the length of the main façade, gives the house its character, and connects the living room with the covered terrace at the extreme right of the plan, as well as with the chapel (shown in detail on page 162).

The family bedrooms and guest rooms are independent of the living area, as well as of the service quarters, which are also arranged around an interior court. A room for the chaplain, with private entrance, is provided at the rear of the chapel.

Taking advantage of the slope of the land, the garages are placed on a lower level, under the terrace at the right of the plan.

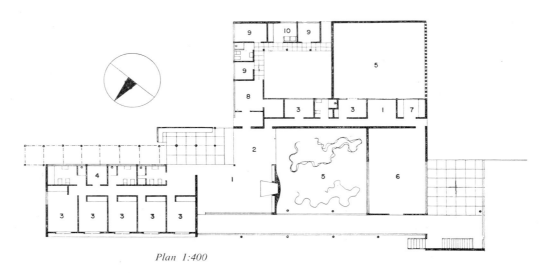

Plan 1:400

1 Living
2 Dining
3 Bedroom
4 Linen
5 Garden
6 Chapel
7 Sacristy
8 Kitchen-Pantry
9 Maid
10 Laundry

Section 1:400

LINA BO BARDI

House for Mr. and Mrs. P. M. Bardi / 1951 / São Paulo

Situated in a new residential suburb of São Paulo, this house is well-suited to its owners, an Italian couple of highly cultivated tastes. Mr. P. M. Bardi, the well-known art critic, helped establish the Museum of Art of São Paulo, and is its director. His wife, a European trained architect, has brought to this house a taste for sophisticated detail and a vocabulary based on an advanced industrial technique.

The house was designed as a minimum of shelter, to make the most of the superb view across the landscape to the great city spread out in the distance. While it protects its occupants adequately from the weather, it still does not interfere with their pleasure in living close to nature, nor of being able to enjoy sunsets and sunrises, even storms and tempests.

The land slopes steeply, so that while the front is supported on *pilotis* the rear part of the house rests on the ground. Contrasting with the massiveness of the rear part, the front appears as the lightest of concrete boxes, with glass on three sides, supported on 'Mannesmann' tubes. In order to accentuate the deliberate thrust toward sky and landscape, there are no protective railings around the large windows of the living room. The patio cuts through the middle of the living room to provide cross ventilation on hot days; an ancient tree, covered with vines and flowers, found on the site, rises from the ground through this patio to become part of the room.

Since the house faces South-southeast, the curtains of white vinylite ('Plavinil') are adequate protection against the morning sun.

A typical finishing detail is the main stairway, a steel structure with granite steps.

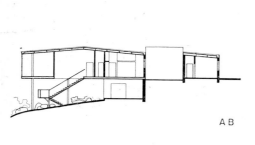

Section 1:500

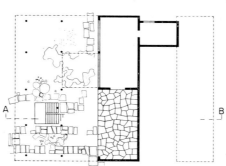

Lower floor 1:500

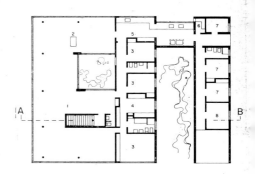

Upper floor 1:500

1 Living-Dining
2 Fireplace
3 Bedroom
4 Dressing room
5 Kitchen-Pantry
6 Wine cellar
7 Maid
8 Linen

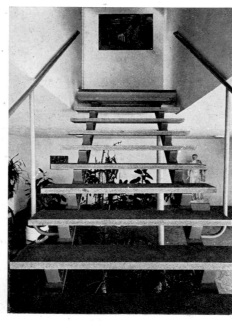

SERGIO W. BERNARDES

House for Jadir de Souza / 1951 / Rio de Janeiro

Almost the opposite of the Bardi house, here it is not a question of a minimum of shelter, but of a plastic and self-sufficient unit, with great refinement of detail, which succeeds in producing, in a lateral garden (sheltered from the street) and in the play of interior volumes, a richness of perspectives scarcely promised by the situation of the lot. A feeling for abstract composition, very character-istic of this architect, disciplines the use of the most varied materials, employed not only for their esthetic effects but for a specific purpose related to the orientation of each part of the building. The subtly detailed millwork precisely accentuates the function of each element of the house.

The garden was done by Carlos Perry.

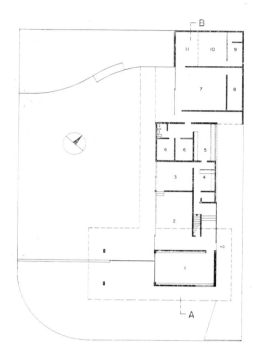

Ground floor 1:500

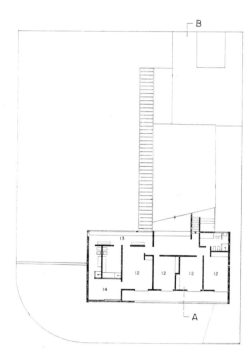

Upper floor 1:500

44

1 Study	8 Storage
2 Living	9 Chauffeur
3 Dining	10 Clothes yard
4 Pantry	11 Laundry
5 Kitchen	12 Bedroom
6 Maid	13 Dressing room
7 Garage	14 Sitting room

Section 1:500

OSWALDO CORRÊA GONÇALVES

House for Osmar Gonçalves / 1951 / Santos, São Paulo

The search for formal composition is also shown in this house, not only by the geometric correlation between the section of *brise-soleil* and the elevation of the main façade, forming similar rectangles, but also in the expression of the method of construction and in the detailing of the openings. The dining and living area (protected from the street by the *brise-soleil* of the terrace) is placed between the sleeping and service wings, and opens onto an intimate patio. This arrangement allows the servants to go from one wing to the other when necessary by way of the patio without being obliged to pass through the living area.

1 Living
2 Dining
3 Bedroom
4 Kitchen-Pantry
5 Maid
6 Laundry
7 Carport

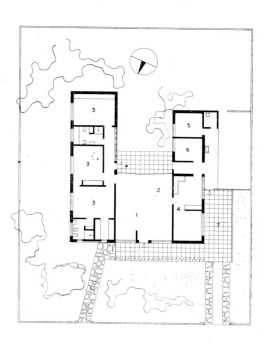

Plan 1:400

OLAVO REDIG DE CAMPOS

House for Ambassador Walther Moreira Salles / 1951 / Rio de Janeiro

Without doubt the costliest residence shown in this book, this house is an example of a program increasingly rare these days: the palatial residence, designed not only to house a family, but also to allow frequent entertaining on a large scale. The architect's Italian background and deliberately exuberant manner incorporate classical European, traditional Brazilian, and strictly contemporary elements into a composition answering these special requirements.

The plan centers around the patio, and opens through a pergola onto the swimming pool set in the garden and surrounded by the landscape dominated by a mountain of living rock.

The living area (reception rooms, library, dining room, galleries and terrace) takes up three sides of the patio and includes a game-room on a lower level, at the fourth side of the patio, below the bedroom wing. The service quarters are at the left, with servants' rooms on the second floor.

The trim of the façades and openings, the marble pavings and balustrades, and every detail set a standard of workmanship, for economic reasons out of the question for most houses.

The gardens were designed by Roberto Burle Marx. They include a tile panel by the same artist and a bronze sculpture by Maria Martins, of a girl playing music on the harplike strings of her hair; the figure slowly rotates, completing the full circle every 24 hours.

Site plan 1:2000

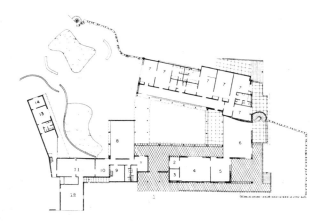

Main floor 1:1000

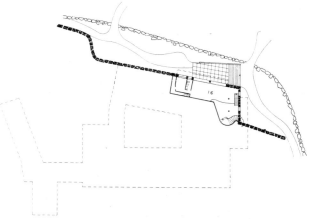

Lower floor 1:1000

1 Cloak room	*9 Linen*
2 Hall	*10 Breakfast room*
3 Safe	*11 Kitchen-Pantry*
4 Library	*12 Garage*
5 Drawing room	*13 Laundry*
6 Living room	*14 Storage*
7 Bedroom	*15 Maid*
8 Dining room	*16 Game room*

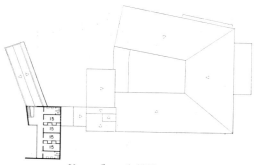

Upper floor 1:1000

SERGIO W. BERNARDES

Country house for Guilherme Brandi / 1952 / Samambáia, near Petrópolis, Rio de Janeiro

The plastic discipline and careful finish of the Jadir de Souza house (page 44), are reaffirmed in this country house which perhaps illustrates even better the architect's search for formal clarity. The simplicity of the composition dominates the variety of textures and materials and shows off the building as a frankly geometric block against the flank of the hill. The treatment of the *pilotis* area, the lightness of the staircase, and the way the stone sustaining wall links house and garden together are carefully designed not to detract from the clean white frame that outlines the main part of the house.

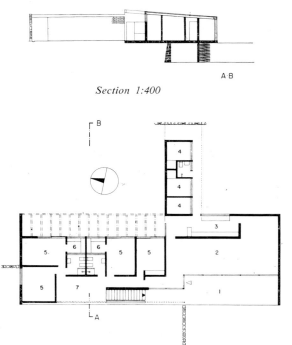

Section 1:400

Main floor 1:400

1 Veranda
2 Living-Dining
3 Kitchen
4 Maid
5 Bedroom
6 Closet
7 Hall

ARNALDO FURQUIM PAOLIELLO

House for Domingos Pires de Oliveira Dias / 1952 / São Paulo

Making use of the slight grade of the lot, this house is designed on three levels. At the right, an intermediate level includes the entrance, living room, dining room and service quarters. At the left are two stories, the lower including the library, winter garden and study and the upper the bedrooms. This arrangement is clearly indicated by the openings of the main façade and the silhouette of the roof, which extends to the right to cover the carport, integrating the whole in one carefully proportioned volume.

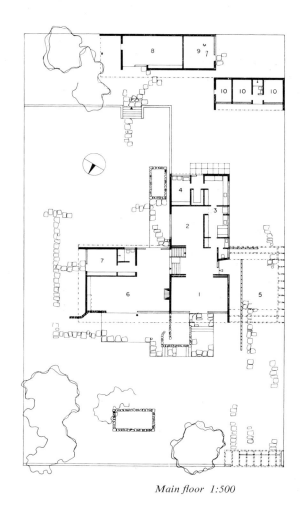

Main floor 1:500

Upper floor 1:500

1 Living room
2 Dining room
3 Kitchen-Pantry
4 Laundry
5 Carport
6 Winter garden and Library
7 Study
8 Games
9 Storage
10 Maid
11 Bedroom
12 Linen

AFFONSO EDUARDO REIDY

House for Miss Carmen Portinho / 1952 / Rio de Janeiro

A permanent residence, and at the same time a refuge from the increasingly difficult urban life of our time, this house was designed for a young woman engineer, actively interested in modern art, who at present is directing the building of the Museum of Modern Art in Rio de Janeiro (page 19), and who, as Chief of the City's Department of Public Housing, was the person most responsible for the carrying out of the Pedregulho project (pages 120–129). The garage and servants' apartment are built directly on the ground, and are joined by the two sides of the sunken patio (which follows the slope of the land) to the main block of the house, raised on *pilotis*. This includes, in an extremely compact plan, a study which can be used as a guest room. The living room extends to the terrace which gives cross ventilation to the bedroom, and where a hammock can be seen, characteristic until today of many parts of Brazil. The *pilotis* structure avoids unnecessary earthmoving. The large glass wall of the living room offers a view of the rich forest vegetation, close to the house, as well as of the vast panorama in the distance.

Plan 1:400

1 Living-Dining
2 Bedroom
3 Study
4 Kitchen
5 Sunken patio
6 Maid
7 Garage

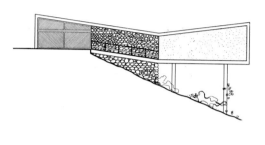

Entrance side elevation 1:400

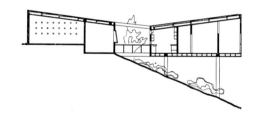

Section 1:400

SERGIO W. BERNARDES

Country house for Miss Lota de Macedo Soares / 1953 / Fazenda Samambáia, near Petrópolis, Rio de Janeiro

Awarded the prize for a house by an architect under forty at the Second Biennial in São Paulo, this house, like the house by Reidy shown on page 54, was designed for a young woman of intellectual and artistic interests who prefers country to city life. Set high up on a mountainside in the Organ Range near Petrópolis, it is a permanent home as well as a place for the entertainment of many guests, frequently friends in the world of contemporary art, both Brazilian and foreign.

The corrugated aluminum roof rests on exposed lattice girders of small iron rods, the struts being welded to the side members in zig-zag pattern and painted black and white, producing an effect of lightness and gaiety. In it the architect has tried to anticipate the steel age, now near at hand in Brazil. The guest rooms and owner's suite are at either end of a long gallery, from which a ramp descends to the entrance, living room, and study, all on a slightly lower level, removed from the kitchen and service area. In this way the occupants are given the maximum privacy and quiet, and the most is made of the dramatic view, changing from room to room. A cascade falls just below the owner's bedroom. In the construction, still going on, the different materials are unified by the discipline of the plastic organization only accented by the play of textures and of the volumes and planes which define each part of the project.

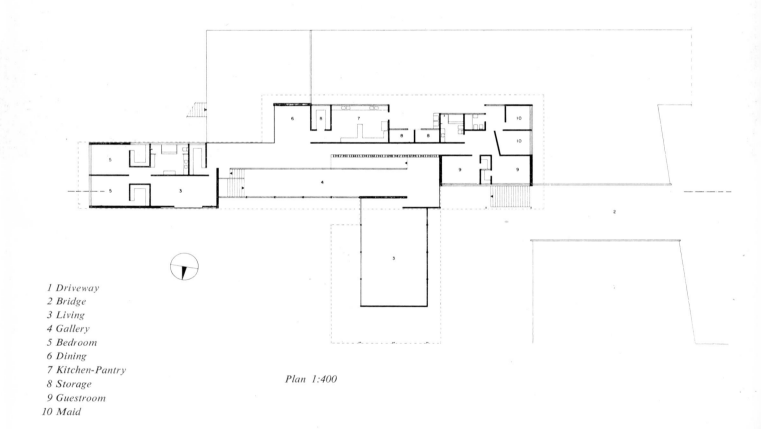

1 Driveway
2 Bridge
3 Living
4 Gallery
5 Bedroom
6 Dining
7 Kitchen-Pantry
8 Storage
9 Guestroom
10 Maid

Plan 1:400

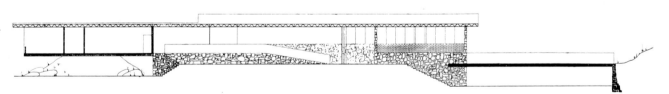

Section 1:400

OSWALDO ARTHUR BRATKE

Studio and Guest Pavilion for house of Oswaldo Arthur Bratke / 1953 / São Paulo

An annex of the architect's residence, this studio was designed as simply as possible as an experiment in the cheapest and most practical methods of construction. Avoiding the rustic and facile picturesque, it makes use of industrial technique that blends discreetly with the polished contemporary style of the main building.

The asphalt roof, with only a 2% slope, is laid over insulating material on a ceiling of wooden planks with exposed beams. Hollow brick, used in the ordinary way in the walls, is very effectively employed in the low screen wall of the terrace where it is laid edgewise so that the openings also provide ventilation.

1 Studio
2 Guest
3 Closet
4 Terrace

Plan 1:400

LYGIA FERNANDES

House for Dr. João Paulo de Miranda Neto / 1953 / Maceió, Alagôas

Situated in Maceió (population 150 000) the capital of Alagôas, a small state in the northeast, this house with its intimate drawing-room, a larger and smaller dining room and sewing room, suggests a way of life rather different to that in the more industrialized parts of the country.

The living room related to the bedroom gallery by the sloping ceiling, the use of *pilotis* in front, and the whole organization of the various elements, belong to a contemporary outlook of design; however, the red terra-cotta tile roof and formally patterned wooden trellises of the veranda in front of the bedrooms again evoke the past, still present so often in Brazilian architecture of today.

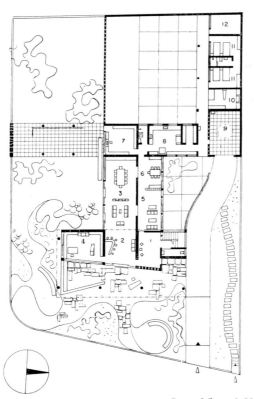

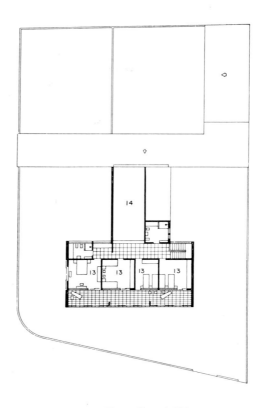

Ground floor 1:500   *Upper floor 1:500*

1 Entry   8 Kitchen-Pantry
2 Living   9 Garage
3 Dining   10 Laundry
4 Study   11 Maid
5 Sitting room   12 Storage
6 Breakfast and lunch   13 Bedroom
7 Sewing room   14 Upper part of Living and Dining room

RINO LEVI *and* ROBERTO CERQUEIRA CESAR
House for Dr. Milton Guper / 1953 / São Paulo

Here the method already used by the architect in his own house (page 26), of protecting glass walls by means of planted boxes shut off by *brise-soleil* in pre-cast concrete, has undergone major development of plastic and functional possibilities, with the happiest results. In this house the patios which correspond to the glass doors are completely covered over with reinforced concrete trellises, forming a kind of light cage beneath which the gardens are sheltered from too much sun and wind. The fusion of interior and exterior obtained in this way, both in the living and dining rooms and in the bedroom gallery, is accentuated by the shadows of the trellises and by the play of light and shade on the floor. The bedrooms have their own patio, used as a playground, and are separated from each other by storage walls of wood, soundproofed with glass wool. The service area (kitchen, pantry, and maid's room) also has its independent patio, partly covered to form a carport. Provisions are delivered directly through the kitchen window. All the rooms have regulated cross ventilation.

The entire area of the building is only about 3230 square feet (300 square meters), or 25% of the lot.

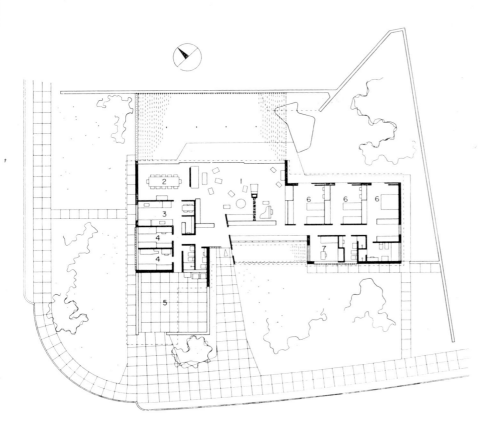

1 Living
2 Dining
3 Kitchen
4 Maid
5 Carport
6 Bedroom
7 Sewing room

Plan 1:400

OSCAR NIEMEYER
House for Oscar Niemeyer / 1953 / Rio de Janeiro

In the vigorous freehand design of the plan, the capricious outline of the roof slab, and the contrast between the curved wall of the living room (paneled in wood) and the wide expanses of glass, this house is characteristic of the personal point of view from which Niemeyer explores the possibilities of new forms and achieves an original plastic vocabulary.

Using the slope of the land to place the bedrooms and a sitting room on a lower level, with a view of the Atlantic Ocean, the living and service areas are arranged on an upper level, opening directly onto the garden; the swimming pool and an enormous granite rock, found on the site, are integrated into the whole.

The roof slab, supported on slender steel posts, and extended to make a shelter near the pool, becomes a part of the sub-tropical landscape itself almost like a natural form. This house represents one facet of the architect's personality already highly developed in the dance hall at Pampulha (page 166) and culminating in the large marquee at Ibirapuéra (page 192).

The sculpture near the swimming pool is by Alfredo Ceschiatti.

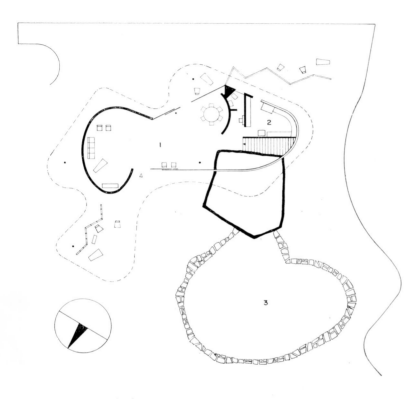

Main floor 1:400

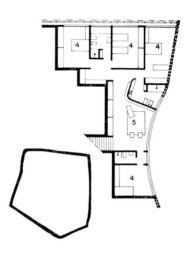

Lower floor 1:400

1 Living-Dining
2 Kitchen-Pantry
3 Swimming pool
4 Bedroom
5 Sitting room

JOSÉ BINA FONYAT FILHO *and* TERCIO FONTANA PACHECO
Country house for João Antéro de Carvalho / 1954 / Parque Rio da Cidade, near Petrópolis, Rio de Janeiro

A peripheral movement, growing out of a tendency towards decentralization already quite noticeable in Rio de Janeiro and São Paulo, results in the fact that a large number of the most interesting houses are found outside the city where larger and less expensive lots of land give the architects better opportunities. It is for this reason that so many of the houses shown in this book are country and vacation houses, or at least are located in suburban areas (as the Bardi, Portinho, Bratke, Niemeyer, Antunes Ribeiro, Waller and Holzmeister houses). As a matter of fact, it is almost easier today to become acquainted with the work of the younger architects by visiting the environs of Petrópolis or Terezópolis than by driving around Rio de Janeiro itself.

In its floor plan and in the treatment of the elevations, this house is representative of the architectural vocabulary and grammar which have been incorporated into Brazilian architecture as a result of earlier research and continued development. The formal composition of the façades, where the different elements fulfill an esthetic purpose as well as the necessary functional one, clearly relates it to contemporary abstract painting, a trend seen fairly often.

The plan consists of two units joined by a gallery. In the first, facing the view, are the living room, dining room and bedrooms. In the second, the service and servants' rooms, as well as a game room, well removed from the bedrooms. Because of the topography of the land it was possible to place the garage beneath the living room, in an area of *pilotis*.

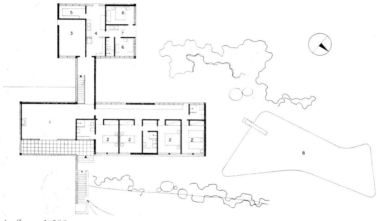

Main floor 1:500

1 *Living-Dining*
2 *Bedroom*
3 *Game room*
4 *Kitchen-Pantry*
5 *Food storage*
6 *Maid*
7 *Laundry*
8 *Swimming pool*

THOMAZ ESTRELLA, JORGE FERREIRA, RENATO MESQUITA DOS SANTOS *and* RENATO SOEIRO

House for Stanislav Kozlowski / 1954 / Rio de Janeiro

This house was designed by the architects who collaborated with Attílio Corrêa Lima in the Seaplane Station (page 224), in the same spirit of restraint and discipline, and it is a good illustration of the difficulties to be overcome in solving the problem of the private house in Rio de Janeiro. The site, increasingly valuable because of its proximity to Leblon Beach and a splendid view of the Atlantic Ocean and the City, was not only relatively cramped but sloped so steeply that mechanical means had to be devised to provide access to the house.

A cable-car climbs to the main floor where the living areas are located. The details of the glass doors connecting the living room to the wide veranda has been carefully worked out, in order to dispense with the usual corner columns. Outside and inside merge completely when the doors are thrown open.

A studio on the lower floor, glazed in front, and three bedrooms on the upper floor also enjoy the magnificent view, which by itself is ample compensation for the difficulties encountered in the construction.

Lower floor 1:500

Main floor 1:500

Upper floor 1:500

1 Study
2 Cable car
3 Storage
4 Living
5 Dining
6 Kitchen-Pantry
7 Laundry
8 Maid
9 Bedroom
10 Closet

RINO LEVI *and* ROBERTO CERQUEIRA CESAR
House for Olivo Gomes / 1954 / São José dos Campos, São Paulo

An enterprising industrialist, for whom Rino Levi designed a workers' housing development, also in São José dos Campos, here gave the architect full opportunity for self expression.

A spirit of research, stripped of preconceptions, and reinforced by fundamental good sense, is joined to pursuit of integration in every detail of construction, finish and furnishing.

Essentially a one-floor house, this house is divided into three distinct units: sleeping quarters, living and service, and servants' rooms. At the back, the house rests directly on the ground, and in front on *pilotis*, making two large covered terraces adjoining the game room and swimming pool. The main entrance is on the upper level, by a hall that separates the living room from the bedroom gallery. The projection of the roof gives shade in summer but admits the low rays of the winter sun. The roof, with insulation as the subject of special study, consists of: an outer roof of corrugated asbestos cement sheets; an air chamber, open around the edges, 21 centimeters (about 8″) deep; a thin slab of hollow brick, and a ceiling sheathed in wood, supported on a reinforced concrete structure.

Because of its exceptional size the living room was especially treated for acoustics. Controlled cross ventilation in all the rooms, a feature of Rino Levi's work, is achieved by lowering the ceilings of the bathrooms and placing fiber cement ventilators in the roof. In the bathrooms light is provided by glass brick ceilings with skylights over them in the roof. The wall at the side of the entrance and the screen wall in the game room are covered with ceramic tiles by Roberto Burle Marx, who also laid out the garden.

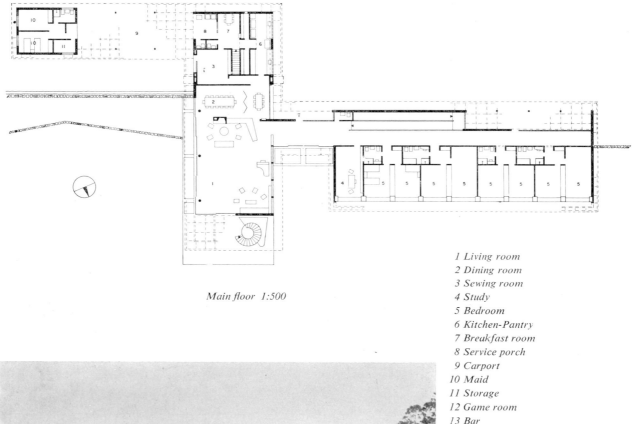

Main floor 1:500

1 Living room
2 Dining room
3 Sewing room
4 Study
5 Bedroom
6 Kitchen-Pantry
7 Breakfast room
8 Service porch
9 Carport
10 Maid
11 Storage
12 Game room
13 Bar

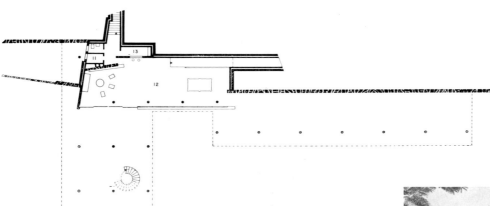

Lower floor 1:500

OLAVO REDIG DE CAMPOS

Country house for Geraldo Baptista / 1954 / Mangalarga, near Petrópolis, Rio de Janeiro

Here, by setting back the bedroom unit in relation to the living and dining rooms, the architect succeeded in placing all the rooms directly on the ground in spite of the steepness of the site. The living areas, service areas, and a three-car garage are on the lower level; on the upper, six bedrooms for the family and guests and the servants' rooms. One patio in the principal bedroom wing, another in the servants' wing, and a third lighting the staircase that connects the two floors, establish the relationship between the house and the garden. On the lower level this relationship is emphasized by the small garden adjoining the dining room, set into the large service court, by the wide sliding doors of the living room and by the covered terrace beside the swimming pool.

Less exuberant than the Moreira Salles house (page 47), although expressed with equal refinement, the formal organization of this house nevertheless shows the architect's characteristic use of masonry and clear delineation of masses.

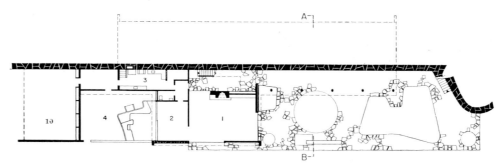

Lower floor 1:500

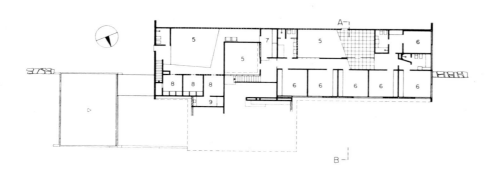

Upper floor 1:500

1 Living
2 Dining
3 Kitchen-Pantry
4 Service court
5 Patio
6 Bedroom
7 Linen
8 Maid
9 Pantry
10 Garage

Section 1:500

PAULO ANTUNES RIBEIRO

House for Paulo Antunes Ribeiro / 1955 / Rio de Janeiro

The discreet composition and apparent simplicity of finish of this house, designed by the architect for himself, conceal the care that has been taken with the proportions of the main floor (3,50 meters, or 11′ 6″ high), and the refined treatment of all the surfaces, from plain white walls, wide expanses of glass in aluminum frames, and variegated floors, to the elaborate ceiling in the living room. This, coffered in a checker-board pattern made possible by concealed V-shaped joists (a technical tour de force) is ideally soundproof, and at the same time gives the room a personal decorative touch.

The particularly uneven lot is situated in a new residential district, in the wooded and mountainous region around Rio de Janeiro. In order not to destroy the character of the land, the entire house is set on *pilotis*. The main floor, considerably larger than the upper one, is partly covered by a wide terrace adjoining the bedrooms and the architect's private study.

A construction by Mario Cravo in the stair well is a little reminiscent of Alexander Calder's visit to Brazil in 1948.

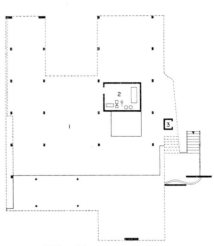

'Pilotis' basement 1:500

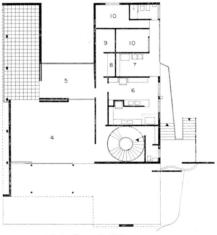

Main floor 1:500

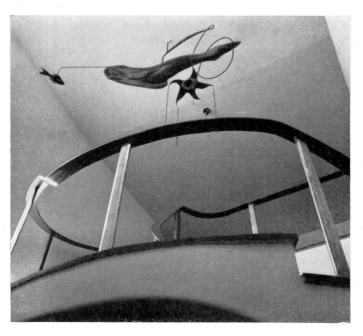

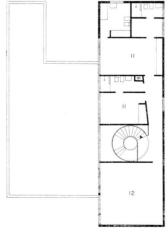

Upper floor 1:500

1 'Pilotis' basement
2 Mechanical equipment
3 Incinerator
4 Living room
5 Dining room
6 Kitchen-Pantry

7 Laundry
8 Air conditioning
9 Storage
10 Maid
11 Bedroom
12 Study

PAULO ANTUNES RIBEIRO

House for Ernesto Waller / 1955 / Rio de Janeiro

This house presented a problem similar to that of the Moreira Salles house (page 47). The topography of the land and the view however suggested a completely different solution. In spite of the very generous program, the composition is extremely restrained. It expands only slightly in the shallow concave line of the roof of the upper floor.

The two-story entrance hall in the middle of the block is approached by a covered driveway beneath the master bedrooms. A circular staircase leads to the bedroom gallery, also reached by a service staircase. The living area (200 square meters, or over 2150 square feet) forms a continuous space in which bookcases mark off

the library and a curved wall the bar. The living room and the bar are 5 meters high (about 16′ 5″). All the living area of the house is closely related to the garden by means of glass walls and sliding doors. Therefore any outside terraces were considered unnecessary.

On the upper floor a large study and a photographic laboratory, with dark room, communicate with the master bedroom.

The servants' rooms and service quarters give an idea of the scale of living for which the house was designed, and it is also implied by the long restful lines of the main elevation, which extends to a length of almost 59 meters (193′).

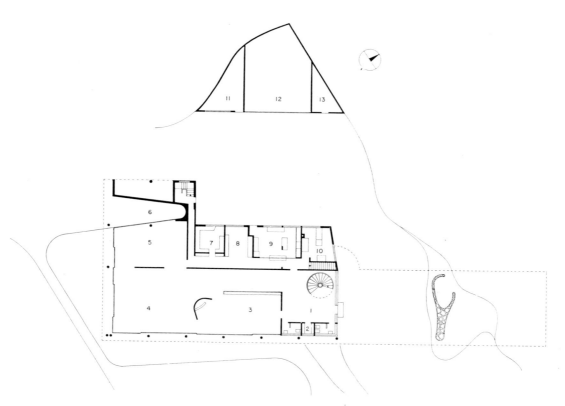

Ground floor 1:500

Site plan 1:2000

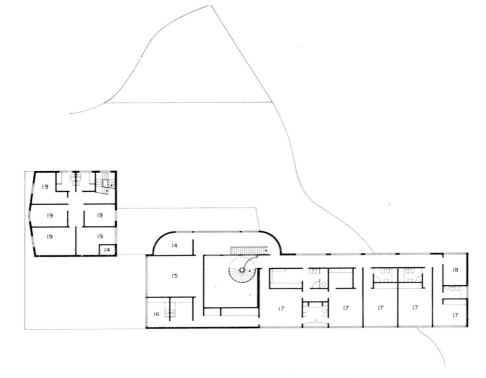

1 Entrance hall
2 Cloak room
3 Library
4 Living
5 Dining
6 Conservatory
7 Food storage
8 Pantry
9 Kitchen
0 Servants' dining room
1 Laundry
2 Garage
3 Storage
4 Air conditioning
5 Study
6 Photographic laboratory
7 Bedroom
8 Linen
9 Maid

Upper floor 1:500

PIRES & SANTOS (Paulo Everard Nunes Pires, Paulo Ferreira dos Santos and Paulo de Tarso Ferreira dos Santos)

House for Martin Holzmeister / 1955 / Rio de Janeiro

This house was built for a nephew of the famous Viennese architect Clemens Holzmeister (born in Brazil of a Brazilian mother). Its architects (one a Professor of Architectural Design and the other Professor of Architecture in Brazil) have tried to achieve the same fusion of traditional and modern elements already seen in the Lúcio Costa house (page 22). It displays the kind of regionalism deserving of more study but still neglected by the majority of architects, although deliberately cultivated by a few, among whom Edgar Graeff, in Rio Grande do Sul, must be cited as an example.

A carefully modulated structure of steel beams and posts (4″ × 4″) permits the façade to be opened up completely, both on the ground floor, all glazed in front, and on the upper floor, poised above the large front veranda.

Everything evokes the past: the formality and generous scale of the plan, the colonial roof of terra cotta tile, the traditionally designed wooden shutters of the bedroom windows, the wide floor boards and the flagstones in the hall. But frank addition of modern elements can be seen throughout, and not only in the technique of construction: in the light iron posts emphasizing the overhang and defining the space of the veranda, in the transparency and openness of the ground floor, in the main staircase, or the sheets of glass used in the upstairs hall parapet.

By placing the house at one side of the site, the larger part of the area could be given over to the garden, designed by Roberto Burle Marx and now being completed.

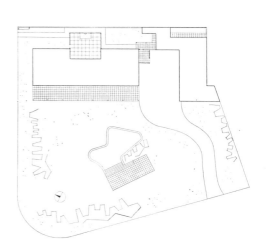

Site plan 1:1000

1 Hall
2 Living room
3 Study
4 Cloak closet
5 Dining room
6 Breakfast room
7 Kitchen-Pantry
8 Cleaning materials
9 Food storage
10 Wine
11 Storage
12 Laundry
13 Maid
14 Playroom
15 Bedroom
16 Dressing room
17 Sitting room
18 Veranda
19 Guest room
20 Closet
21 Housekeeper
22 Linen

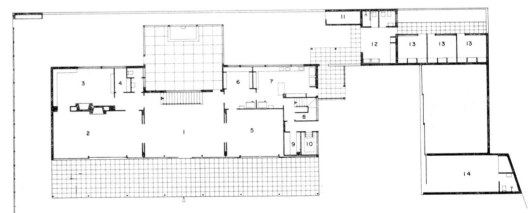

Ground floor 1:400

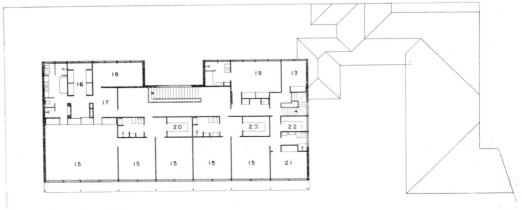

Upper floor 1:400

MIGUEL FORTE *and* GALIANO CIAMPAGLIA
House for Luiz Forte / 1955 / São Paulo

In this house another attempt has been made to blend the old and the new, though in a less regional manner than in the Holzmeister house. Especially adapted to its site is the uncommon arrangement of the usual elements of the plan. The vigorously delineated structure restricts the relative exuberance with which the various materials are used and also expresses the intention of the design, essentially organic and yet avoiding any narrow orthodox viewpoint.

The dining room and service areas are on the second floor, on the level of the bedrooms, so that the service patio rests directly on the highest part of the lot. On the lower level are the garage, study, and living area. This, organized as a continuous space in which the furnishings are a part of the architectural plan, consists of a living room and covered terrace on the lowest level; three steps higher, the entrance hall, a gallery, and the bar. The patio-corridor on the south side, sheltered by a pergola, is planted as a garden and contains an ornamental fishpond. The servants' rooms are over the laundry, in the service area.

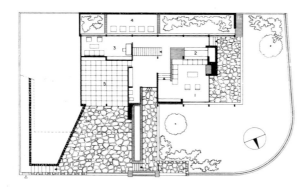

Lower floor 1:500

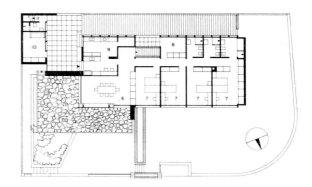

Upper floor 1:500

1 Living room
2 Bar
3 Study
4 Ornamental fishpond
5 Garage
6 Dining room
7 Bedroom
8 Linen
9 Kitchen-Pantry
0 Laundry
1 To servants' rooms above

Country house for Lauro de Souza Carvalho / 1955 / Samambáia, near Petrópolis, Rio de Janeiro

The land on which this country house is built dominates the entrance to Fazenda Samambáia, where the Brandi and Lota de Macedo Soares residences (page 50 and 56) are located, and extends westward in a ravine down which the Rio Piabanha leaps in a narrow cascade on its way to Petropolis. The house, set crosswise to valley, enjoys a fine view in either direction: the stream on the one hand and, to the east, the restful panorama of the hills stretching up and away to the mountains in the distance.

The living area, which includes the living, dining and game rooms, is connected to the garden by the front terrace and protected on the opposite side by a spacious veranda; with the car port underneath, it seems poised in space. Below the bedroom wing, which runs along the very edge of the slope, are the servants' quarters located on a level with the carport.

The contrasting elements of the design—the reinforced concrete structure, the brick walls, exposed or plastered, the millwork and ceilings, in rough-hewn wood or smooth floor-boarding, as well as the varying color-scheme—are freely used to accentuate a lack of formality, providing a suitable background for rest and relaxation.

The garden, now being made, was planned by Burle Marx.

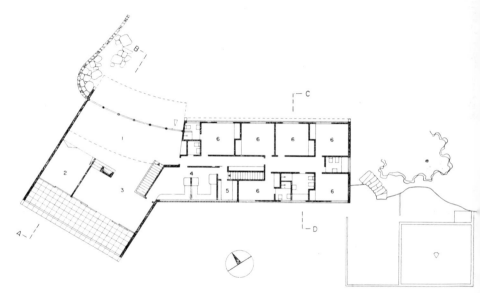

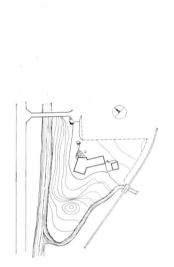

Site plan 1:4000   Main floor 1:400

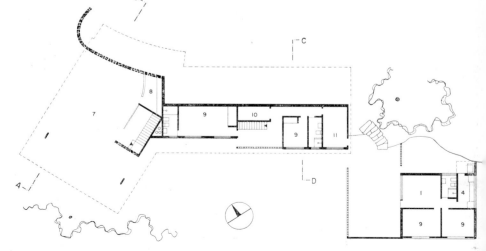

1 Living room
2 Card room
3 Dining room
4 Kitchen-Pantry
5 Food storage
6 Bedroom
7 Carport
8 Storage
9 Maid
10 Mechanical equipment
11 Laundry

Lower floor 1:400

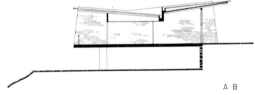

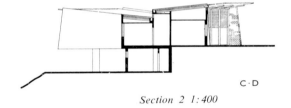

A·B

C·D

Section 1 1:400

Section 2 1:400

ALVARO VITAL BRAZIL *and* ADHEMAR MARINHO
Edificio 'Esther' / 1938 / São Paulo

This office and apartment building, the first large building with an independent structure completed in Brazil, created an enormous sensation because of the novelties it introduced, among which were the free-standing columns in the middle of the rooms. Many tenants requested permission to remove them from their apartments, promising to restore them to their places at the termination of the lease.

Instead of spreading in the conventional way over the whole lot, it was placed on the site so as to permit a new street to be cut through parallel to the front of the edifice, which thus remains free on all four sides. The rear of the lot could then be used for a smaller building which can be seen in the photograph, behind the larger one. The free structure of regularly ordered columns (although the spacing is less than it would be today) facilitated a variety of floor plans. Thus the ground floor, besides various circulation arcades, includes a large area for shops; the 2nd, 3rd, and 4th floors, office space divided as desired; the 5th, one or two room apartments; the 6th, 7th, 8th, and 9th, two or three bedroom apartments, with kitchens and maids' rooms; the 10th and 11th include four duplex apartments; and finally the top floor is taken up by two penthouse apartments, surrounded by terraces.

The basement garage covers not only the area of the building but extends under the new street referred to above. The service facilities of the apartments are placed around four light wells which begin at the 5th floor.

In this pioneer work, that has retained its value because of its functional organization, the architectural treatment of the façades, accented by strips of black vitrolite, and clearly expressing the structure and the variety of the plans, should be observed.

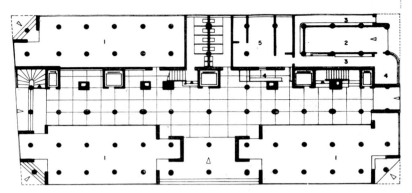

Ground floor 1:400

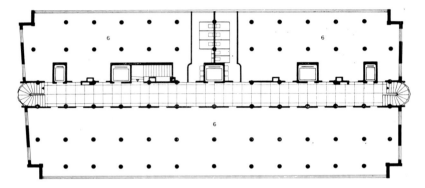

Second, third and fourth floor 1:400

1 Shop
2 Service and Garage entrance
3 Light and gas meters
4 Doorman
5 Janitor
6 Office area (partitioned at will)
7 Living-Dining
8 Bedroom
9 Kitchen
10 Food storage
11 Laundry tub and Maid's W.C.
12 Storage
13 Upper part of Living room

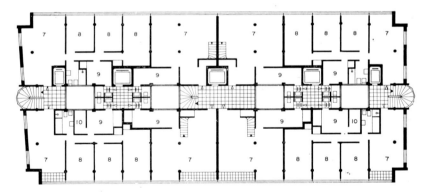

Tenth floor 1:400

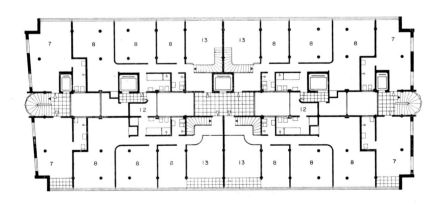

Eleventh floor 1:400

GREGORI WARCHAVCHIK
Apartment building / 1939 / São Paulo

This building, which attempts to lessen the feeling of confinement of a small apartment by openness and by an imaginative touch, sums up many of the problems due to small, narrow building sites, the bugbear of Brazilian architects. The high price of land demands that it be used to maximum advantage; the architect, unable to influence a project already poor in itself from the human and city-planning point of view, can only restrain the speculators' ambition and try to impose his own order and clarity.

The abundance of domestic help, already mentioned, introduces elements less common in other countries: servants' rooms and independent circulation for the service. In this building, however, in order to enable tenants of modest means to rent compact apartments, Warchavchik has dispensed with both these requirements. The apartments are of two types: those at the front with living room and two bedrooms; and at the back, one-room, with an alcove for the bed.

1 Living-Dining
2 Bedroom
3 Kitchen
4 Sleeping alcove

Typical floor 1:500

HELIO UCHÔA

Luiz Felipe' apartment house / 1945 / Rio de Janeiro

Here again the architect has had to apply resource and ingenuity to the problem of meeting the limitations imposed by excessive sub-division of the land, and yet provide apartments as well lit and efficiently planned as conditions will allow.
The ground floor, taken up by the entrance and the janitor's quarters, has a front garden that helps to give a lighter appearance to the building block. The façade, framed in a white molding, is faced with blue ceramic mosaic tile, and the balconies are finished in white plaster,

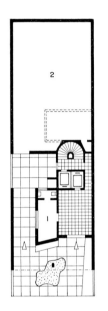

Ground floor 1:400   *Typical floor 1:400*

1 Doorman
2 Garage
3 Living-Dining
4 Kitchen-Pantry
5 Maid
6 Bedroom
7 Linen

87

M. M. M. ROBERTO

Apartment house in Botafogo / 1947 / Rio de Janeiro

In these apartments (built for the employees of one of the retirement and pensions funds which are the basic elements of the system of workers' insurance and social welfare in Brazil) a special effort was made to combine cross ventilation and double exposure in each dwelling unit along with the requirements already mentioned: keeping the service circulation apart from the main circulation. To this end, the two levels common to the basic duplex type (entry and living-and-dining room, kitchen, maid's bedroom and toilet, on the lower floor; three bedrooms and bathroom on the upper floor) have been ingeniously alternated with the levels of the tenants' and service corridors, themselves alternating one above the other. The main corridor, for the use of the tenants, runs four steps below the lower floor of the duplex and provides access to this floor only. The service corridor, however, communicates with both floors, being six steps below the bedroom floor and eleven steps above the living room floor. This difference in levels raises the ceiling height of the service corridor, allowing the rear window of both floors to open onto it, instead of onto the main corridor—the back bedroom and bathroom at the top and the kitchen, maid's room and toilet at the bottom. Interior communication between the two levels of the apartment is obtained by means of a staircase with two flights, one longer than the other, and a landing on a level with the service corridor, but separated from it by a small passage with a laundry sink. Thus it is possible to reach the bedroom floor and the lower floor from the service corridor by going up six steps or down eleven, without passing by the living room. Alternate units in the smaller block have separate service stairways winding up from the kitchen to the upper level of the duplexes.

The loggias two floors high, looking out over Guanabara Bay, characterize the duplex scheme of the project in plastic terms.

The irregularity of the land was responsible for the division of the whole into two blocks, connected only by the circulation galleries to the elevator tower located on the lower part of the site.

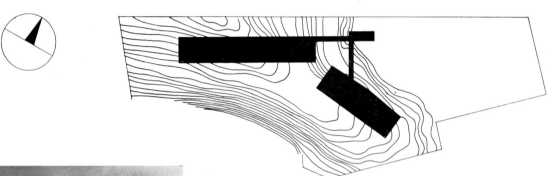

Site plan 1:2000

Section 1:1000

1 Living-Dining
2 Kitchen
3 Maid
4 Bedroom
5 Linen
6 Service

Typical duplex, lower level 1:400
Typical duplex, upper level 1:400

Alternate unit, lower level 1:400
Alternate unit, upper level 1:400

Section detail, alternate unit 1:400

LÚCIO COSTA

'Nova Cintra', 'Bristol' and 'Caledonia' apartment buildings in Eduardo Guinle Park / 1948-1950-1954 / Rio de Janeiro

The Eduardo Guinle Park is a new residential development a short distance from the center of Rio de Janeiro. It is located on the grounds of a mansion built in 1916, now used as the official residence of the President of the Republic, and some adjacent land which was taken over. It will consist of six apartment buildings (three of which are completed at the present time) and a number of lots for individual houses. The entire project is to be built according to an all over plan in which no expense is being spared. The project's having been promoted with personal interest by the heirs of Eduardo Guinle, the original owner, undoubtedly contributed to the liberality with which the plan was designed.

The first building (Nova Cintra) faces the main street leading to the park, and the other two (Bristol and Caledonia) are on a new street cut through the property and leading to the individual lots further on. The desire to keep intact as much of the park as possible, resulted in the Bristol and Caledonia buildings, although enjoying the best view, being rather unfavorably oriented. However, this disadvantage was minimized by the treatment of the façades,

in which fixed *brise-soleil* and panels of pierced tile-work result in plays of texture and of light and shade very characteristic of this phase of Brazilian architecture.

The three apartments are built with freestanding structures that permit the greatest flexibility of floor plans, and each contains apartments of various sizes, including a series of duplexes. With the exception of the façades of Bristol and Caledonia, the three buildings are essentially the same. Therefore only the plans of Nova Cintra are reproduced here. In this building there are shops on the ground floor, and the garage is behind the block, in two levels. The other buildings have *pilotis* on the ground floor and garages in the basements. The top floors consist of penthouse apartments. The area of each apartment varies from 225 to 515 square meters (about 2420 to 5540 sq. ft.) in net area, or 286 to 604 square meters (about 3080 to 6500 sq. ft.) in gross area, i.e., including the cooperatively owned area of the common use facilities. In the first Biennial of the Museum of Modern Art in São Paulo (1951), these buildings received the first prize for apartment houses.

1 Nova Cintra building
2 Bristol building
3 Caledonia building
4 Future buildings
5 Forest preserve
6 Park and Playground
7 Small lake
8 Old mansion
9 Paulo César de Andrade street
10 Gago Coutinho street
11 Laranjeiras street

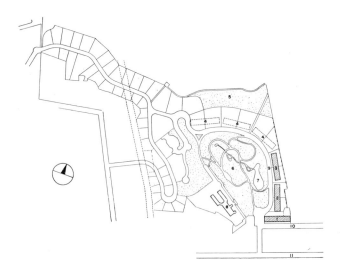

General Plan 1:10000

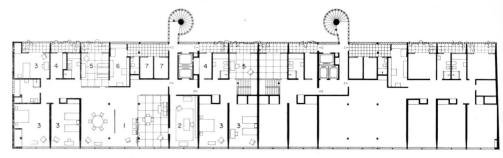

Fourth, sixth and eighth floor 1:500

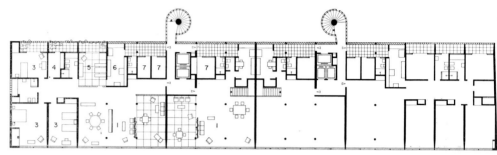

Third, fifth and seventh floor 1:500

1 Living-Dining
2 Study
3 Bedroom
4 Linen
5 Veranda
6 Kitchen-Pantry
7 Maid
8 Restaurant
9 Freight
10 Pantry
11 Shop
12 Doorman
13 Garage

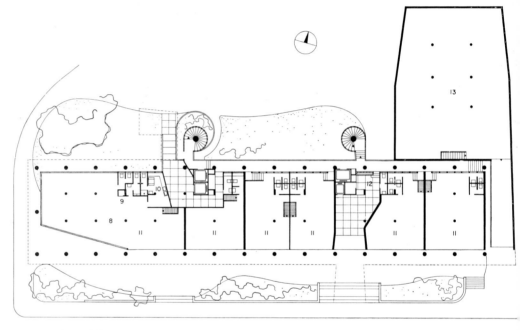

Ground floor 1:500

A Type 'A' apartments
B Type 'B' apartments
C Type 'C' apartments
D Type 'D' apartments

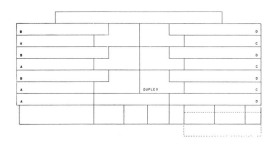

Schematic section 1:1000

93

J. VILANOVA ARTIGAS

'Louveira' apartment buildings / 1950 / São Paulo

The two units are placed on the lot to give the living rooms and bedrooms as much sunlight as possible. The distance between them is determined by the city building code requirement that sunrays touch the patio for a certain period of time on the shortest day of the year (see page 10). Avoiding the conventional arrangement along the two street fronts, the plan leaves the two units completely separate with no enclosed court, and a large garden and turn-around patio between them. The light, gay, entrance ramp connecting them divides the garden from the turnaround and contrasts pleasantly with the quiet elevations of the buildings. The servic[e] hallways are five steps below the level of each floor to save spac[e] for communication between the main elevator and the servic[e] elevator. This communication, which for safety reasons should b[e] compulsory in all buildings of this type, would reduce the width [of] the dining room too much unless handled in this way. To avoid [a] view of the service quarters from the rear building the galleries ar[e] covered with wire screens. The bedroom windows are similar t[o] those of the Artigas house in Santos (page 34).

Typical floor 1:500

1 Living
2 Dining
3 Terrace
4 Bedroom
5 Kitchen
6 Maid
7 Entrance hall
8 Service
9 Car and service entrance
10 Turnaround

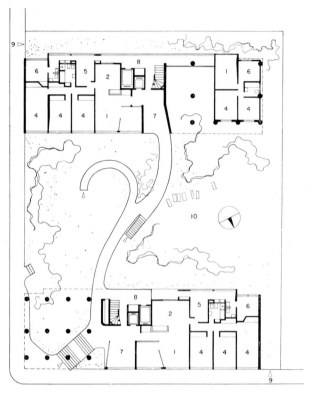

Entrance floor 1:500

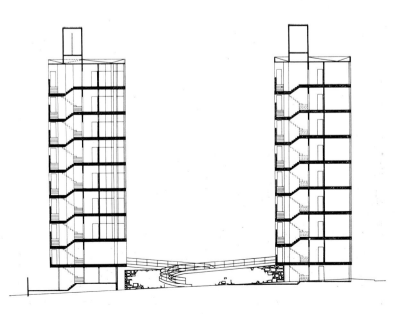

Section 1:500

RINO LEVI *and* ROBERTO CERQUEIRA CESAR

'Prudencia' apartment building / 1950 / São Paulo

Built to sell under the cooperative-ownership scheme now so prevalent in Brazil, this luxury class apartment house in a residential section near the center of the city incorporates many desirable features, inside and out, in its detail and its equipment. This includes complete air-conditioning and sound-proofing, and a private elevator for each apartment besides the service elevators, one to each two apartments.

The land, about 265′ long by 165′ deep (or about 80 by 50 meters) is almost 10 feet (3 meters) above the street and has an excellent view over the city. The ground floor with *pilotis* contains the entrances and a playground, and partly covers a garage under-ground, with separate ramps to the street for cars and pedestrians. There are nine stories of four apartments each, 400 square meters (about 4,300 sq. ft.) and two penthouses on the top floor, 450 square meters (about 4,850 sq. ft.). The façades are covered with small porcelain tiles, 2 × 2 cm. (about 3/4 × 3/4″) in blue, brown and yellow.

The complete flexibility of the arrangement of living rooms and bedrooms, the result of the type of structure adopted, is demonstrated by the layout plans A, B, C, and D, which show the variations possible.

1 *Living-Dining*
2 *Bedroom*
3 *Study*
4 *Kitchen-Pantry*
5 *Maid*
6 *Bath*
7 *Tenants' elevator*
8 *Service elevator*
9 *Hall*
10 *Doormen*
11 *Ramps to basement*
12 *Pedestrians' ramp*
13 *Playground*

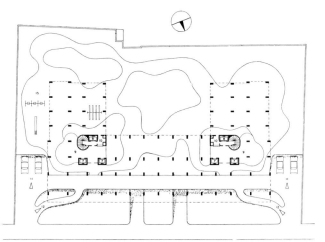

round floor 1:1000

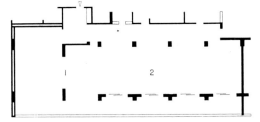

ayout scheme A 1:400

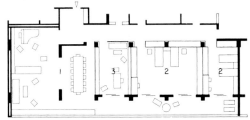

ayout scheme B 1:400

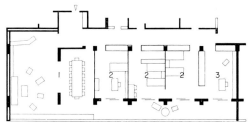

ayout scheme C 1:400

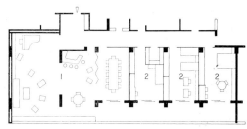

Layout scheme D 1:400

Half of typical floor 1:400

HENRIQUE E. MINDLIN

'Três Leões' apartment building / 1951 / São Paulo

An original solution was adopted in this design to solve the problem of providing separate access to the front and back doors of the apartments without unduly increasing the number of elevators and restricting the valuable space available on the lower floors for the shop and offices of the firm that owns the building. This solution consisted of alternating tenants' and servants' corridors, and placing them between floors, where they are served respectively by two elevators rising from the main entrance hall on the ground floor, and two from the basement reached by the service entrance at the side of the building. A few steps up or down connect the corridors to the apartment levels. The corridors used by the tenants are 2.50 meters (8′ 2½″) high and fully enclosed, while those for service use are 3.50 meters (11′ 6″) in height and look out over a low parapet onto a large inner courtyard lighting the kitchens and bathrooms. The nine lower floors, each with eleven apartments, have six independent staircases. In the eight-story tower, with four apartments on each floor, the two staircases are shifted to one side of those on the lower floors in order to save space. The terraces and balconies, alternating from floor to floor to get more winter sunshine, are located either in front of the living room or of the bedroom; this insures the preferences of the tenants,—those without children favoring the bedroom terrace, in order to have a larger living room.

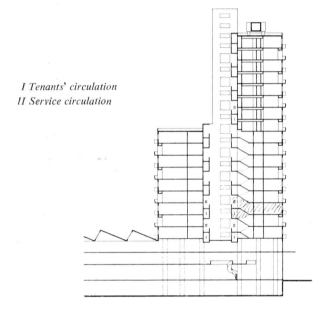

I Tenants' circulation
II Service circulation

General section 1:1000

1 Living
2 Bedroom
3 Bachelor apartment

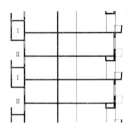

Detail section 1 1:500

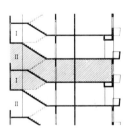

Detail section 2 1:500

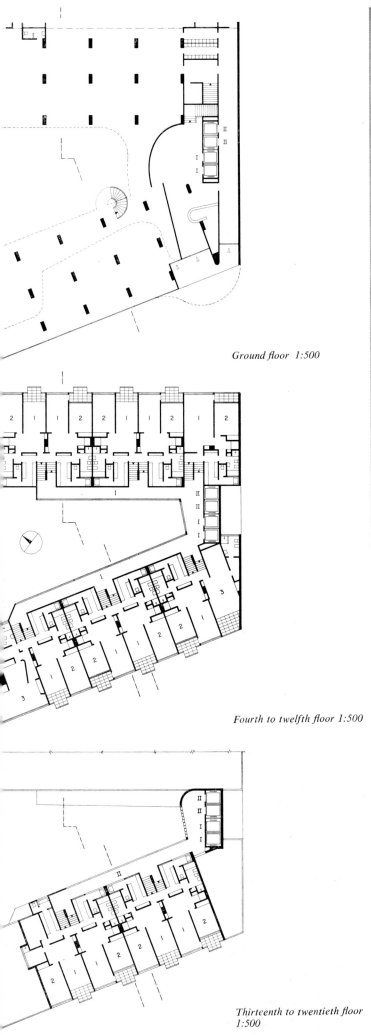

Ground floor 1:500

Fourth to twelfth floor 1:500

Thirteenth to twentieth floor
1:500

JORGE MACHADO MOREIRA
'Antonio Ceppas' apartment building / 1952 / Rio de Janeiro

In this building erected on the hillside, with a front view over the Rodrigo de Freitas Lagoon and a back view of the City forest reserve, the crowding of the site is compensated by the *pilotis* area on the ground floor which is almost entirely open and has a playground at the back. There are four apartments on each of the six upper floors and all the rooms have a view, with the exception of the kitchens and maids' bedrooms and toilets, which look out into inner court-yards as a result of the limitations imposed on the architect by the high cost of the lot. Advantage has been taken of the slope of the land and of the street to locate the garages in the basement. Access to the ground floor is by a broad stone staircase with a marquee overhead. The service entrance leads off the City steps and passage on the right.

Extreme care taken in the design of the millwork, interpreting functional requirements in subtle combination with traditional and contemporary elements, has produced elevations that are distinctly regional in character. The bedroom terraces in front are protected by wooden trellises, which confer a cozy intimacy without interfering with the view. Similar trellises at the top of the living room windows are combined with horizontally sliding sashes in the middle and swiveling wooden louvers at the bottom. The bedroom windows are also provided with top ventilation by means of swiveling or pivoting wooden louvers.

All the millwork is painted white except the trellises, which are yellow. The building itself is pearl gray. The panels of the lateral façades are painted blue, and the marquee and moldings on the front and rear façades are faced with blue mosaic. The *pilotis* area was landscaped by Roberto Burle Marx, who also designed the glass mosaic panel near the ornamental basin and the two cement tile murals between the entrances to the two main halls.

The Antonio Ceppas building won an honorable mention at the Second Biennial of São Paulo, held in 1953.

1 *Living*
2 *Dining*
3 *Bedroom*
4 *Kitchen*
5 *Maid*

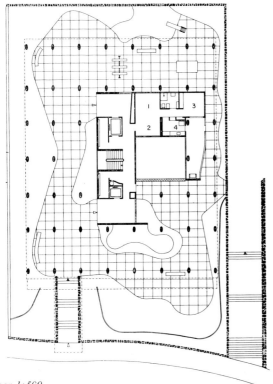

Ground floor 1:500

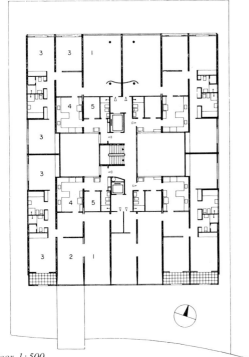

Typical floor 1:500

PLINIO CROCE *and* ROBERTO AFLALO

'Biaçá' apartment building / 1953 / São Paulo

This building forms one unit of a housing project comprising apartments for lease to tenants in the middle income brackets. The architects were appointed by the owner, a large real estate and mortgage bank, in accordance with the results of a competition. The scheme adopted to take advantage of the unevenness of the site has been expressed in compact, straightforward plans and equally conscientious elevations.

The floors of the rear block are half a story higher than those of the front one, so that the halls of each two apartments open onto one of the alternate landings of the staircase that joins the two blocks. Each block has six garages on the ground floor corresponding to the two apartments on each of the three upper stories. The entrances are on one side of the building in passageways giving access to the back of the garages, each with its own door. The areas admitting light to the kitchens and bathrooms, and to the staircase, are open on one side; the maids' bedrooms and bathrooms are less reminiscent than usual of the days of slavery and have outside windows.

The bedroom windows are of the counterbalancing sash type (as on page 35), but the frames are faced inside and out with tongue-and-groove floorboarding. The façades are finished in white hexagon mosaic tile.

102

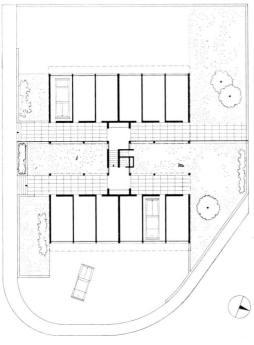

Ground floor 1:500

Typical floor 1:500

1 *Living-Dining*
2 *Bedroom*
3 *Maid*

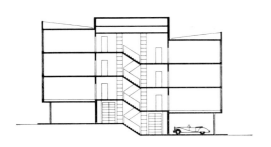

Section 1:500

OSCAR NIEMEYER

'Grande Hotel' / 1940 / Ouro Preto, Minas Gerais

The little town of Ouro Preto, former capital of Minas Gerais, is a veritable museum of eighteenth century architecture. It is now preserved as a national monument by the *Serviço do Patrimônio Histórico e Artístico Nacional*, for the winding streets evoke memories of Tiradentes, the first martyr in the cause of independence, and the many churches provide examples of the sculpture of Aleijadinho, the foremost artist of the colonial period.

Yet this thoroughly up-to-date hotel with its 20 single rooms, 7 double rooms and 17 duplex suites fits marvelously into a landscape of bygone days without having to rely on any copying of obsolete styles to do so.

The mass of the building is spread out horizontally, only four stories high. The colonial-tile roof, the wooden trellis-work on the terraces, the facing of stone and *azulejos*, and the characteristic coloring, help to harmonize the building with the surroundings. Lightness is given to the construction by extending the *pilotis* up to the third floor.

The ground floor is taken up by the kitchen and offices, and there is also a playroom and a large covered terrace. A ramp leads up to the second floor where the restaurant and other public rooms are to be found. The third floor is divided by a central corridor, with the single and double rooms in the back of the building and the living rooms of the duplexes in the front, each with a circular staircase leading up to the bedroom and bathroom, and with a private sun porch.

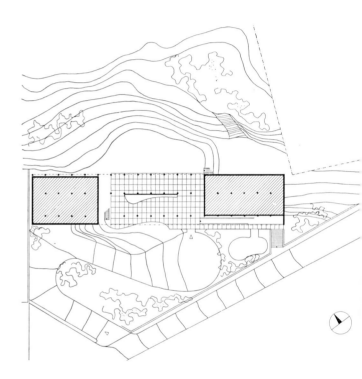

Site plan 1:1000

1 Game room
2 Kitchen
3 Laundry
4 Maid
5 Front office
6 Lounge
7 Writing room
8 Reading room
9 Exhibitions
0 Dining room
1 Pantry
2 Service
3 Bedroom
4 Living room
5 Upper part of living room
6 Balcony

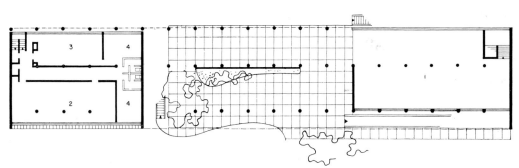

Ground floor 1:500

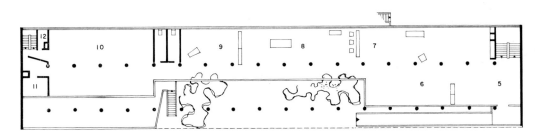

Second floor 1:500

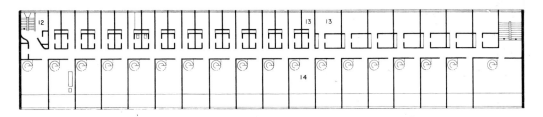

Third floor 1:500

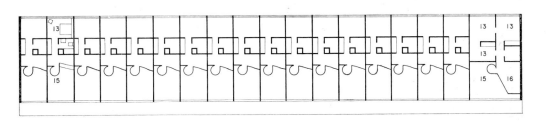

Fourth floor 1:500

LÚCIO COSTA

'Park Hotel' / 1944 / Parque São Clemente, Friburgo, Rio de Janeiro

Fusion with the environment, embodying emotional relationship with the past, yet free of any slavish urge to copy or imitate, and hence leaving the way clear for the adoption of characteristic contemporary solutions, is carried even further in this project.

On a mountainside in the Organ Range, 2800 feet above sea level, this hotel with only ten rooms caters to a luxury vacation park, organized by the promotors of Parque Eduardo Guinle (page 90). The extremely rustic construction employing local materials is en-

hanced by the large windows on the lower floor, by the movable wooden *brise-soleil* of the children's playroom, and by the glazed sliding doors with louvers in the upper part leading from each bedroom onto a private sun porch.

The kitchen and offices are in the lowest wing and the cellar is in the basement underneath the restaurant. The bathrooms are lighted by a clerestory over the corridor.

1 Veranda
2 Lounge
3 Dining room
4 Kitchen
5 Linen
6 Maid
7 Employees' sitting room
8 Boiler
9 Employees' dining room
10 Manager
11 Playroom
12 Bedroom
13 Storage

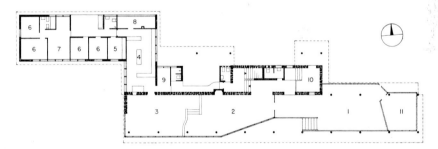

Lower floor 1:500

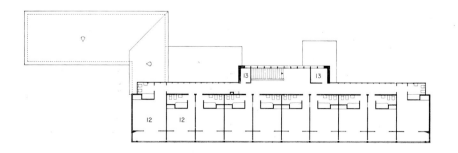

Upper floor 1:500

107

M. M. ROBERTO

Week-end and vacation hostel / 1944 / Rio de Janeiro

Although the influence of the past is not so strong in this case as in the previous example, a deliberate attempt has been made to reconcile traditional elements with a reinforced concrete structure in a new design. The hostel was built to accomodate employees of the I R B (see page 202) at weekends and on vacation, and is situated in the forest that surrounds Rio de Janeiro on a site where a large area is available for sports and recreation.

The hostel can accomodate 31 guests on vacation and 52 weekend visitors in dormitories and a certain number of private rooms. The slope of the site made it possible for the first two floors to be at ground level on opposite sides. Access to the lower is from the south, and here are the service rooms, as well as a children' playroom. The main or second floor, with access from the north contains the lounge and games rooms, dining room, bar and kitchen, and, on the southern side, is connected with the park by large projecting terrace and by two wide openings on the lounge area. The dormitories and private rooms are on the top floor, the dressing-rooms and bathrooms being lit by clerestories above the outside corridor.

Economy in construction work and finish, imposed by the very nature of the project is revealed in every detail, including the exposed beams and joists of the structure.

Section 1:1000

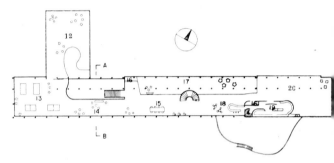

Main floor 1:1000

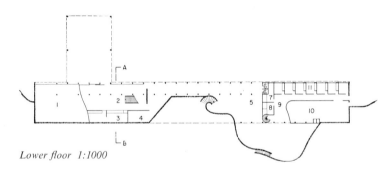

Lower floor 1:1000

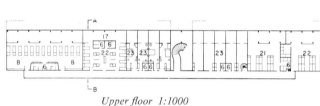

Upper floor 1:1000

1 Garage
2 Entrance
3 Manager
4 Barber
5 Recreation
6 W.C.
7 Men's lockers
8 Women's lockers
9 Service hall
10 Laundry
11 Servant's room
12 Terrace
13 Games – billiards, table tennis
14 Lounge
15 Reading room
16 Bell captain
17 Veranda
18 Bar
19 Kitchen
20 Dining room
21 Girls' dormitory
22 Boys' dormitory
23 Private room

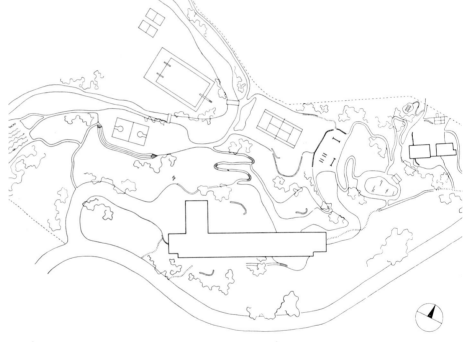

Site plan 1:2000

PAULO ANTUNES RIBEIRO *and* DIOGENES REBOUÇAS

'Hotel da Bahia' / 1951 / Salvador, Bahia

Completely different in character is this 180-room hotel, which provides a strikingly modern contrast in the capital of the state of Bahia, that prides itself on a wealth of historic buildings and a hundred old churches.

The project embodies up-to-date ideas in hotel management and comprises: service rooms in the basement; a grillroom, night club and five small shops on the ground floor; and an ample lounge, restaurant and kitchen on the second floor. Five stories for rooms, each with 36 units, have been built, though the original project called for eight bedroom floors bringing the total up to 270 units. An intermediate floor between room floors and public floors is used to centralize plumbing and soil stacks. The room windows are fitted with louvered shutters, sliding horizontally, and the stair-

case is protected by a screenwork of hollow circular tile arranged s as to form an hexagonal pattern. The spacing of the columns, whic differs in the two halves of the plan to facilitate the layout of th public rooms, is clearly shown in the elevations of the lower floor Departing therein from the discipline of the upper block, the publ rooms feature a somewhat exuberant variety of atmosphere len ing itself to interior decoration. This is in line with the commerci: nature of the undertaking, which seeks to attract the tourist i search of novelty and the thrill of living in a different environmen The decorative tiling with motifs in relief was designed by Paul Antunes Ribeiro and the 4×50 meter ($13' \times 164'$) mural in th regional-style restaurant is the work of Genaro Carvalho.

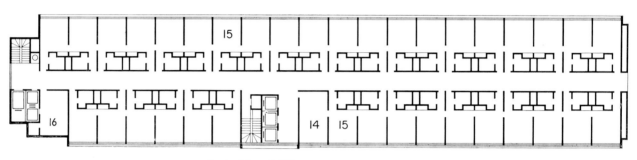

Typical floor 1:500

1 Front office
2 Telephones
3 Shop
4 Grill and night club
5 Bar
6 Pantry
7 Management
8 Boiler
9 Lounge
10 Dining room
11 Chef
12 Kitchen
13 Exhaust
14 Sitting room
15 Bedroom
16 Room service

110

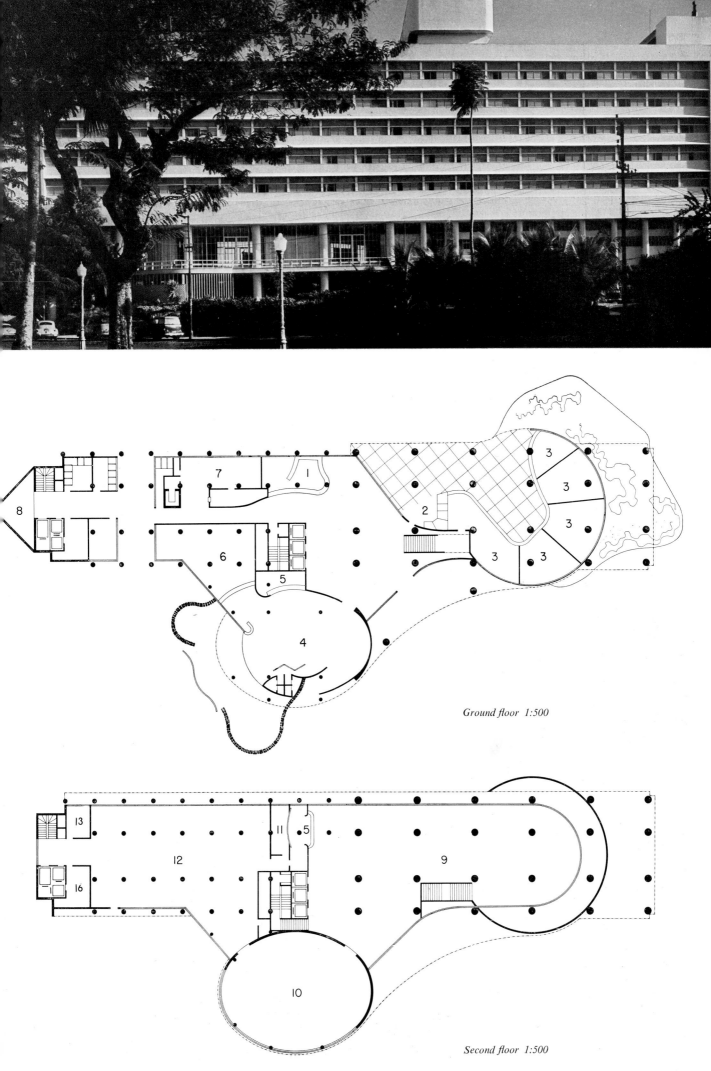

Ground floor 1:500

Second floor 1:500

Staff housing, Type 'A', for the Aeronautical Technical Center (Centro Técnico de Aeronautica) / 1947 / São José dos Campos, São Pau

The Aeronautical Technical Center, now nearing completion, is located some 68 miles to the northeast of São Paulo, not far from the Dutra Highway, which connects this city to Rio de Janeiro. It will comprise a school block, laboratories, training workshops and an airport, in addition to a housing development for about 4000 people, including teachers, personnel and students. Various types of dwellings, already built, are illustrated on the next few pages. The richness of variation around a central theme that the architect

has succeeded in obtaining not only gives plastic interest to t whole, but human significance to each unit.

Type 'A' block comprises 16 dwellings on the ground floor a 20 on the upper story, to which access is provided by a galle with two large circular staircases. The service area on the top flo is lighted by an opening in the roof.

Each unit contains two bedrooms, as well as a maid's room cl to the service area.

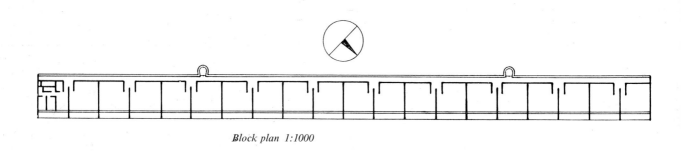

Block plan 1:1000

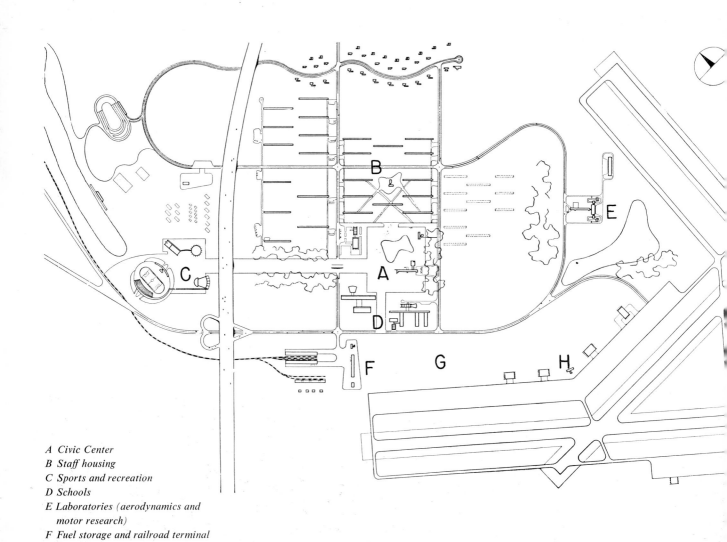

A Civic Center
B Staff housing
C Sports and recreation
D Schools
E Laboratories (aerodynamics and
   motor research)
F Fuel storage and railroad terminal
G Auxiliary buildings
H Military airport

Living-Dining
Kitchen
Maid
Bedroom
Service yard

ower floor 1:400   Upper floor 1:400   Section 1:400

OSCAR NIEMEYER

Staff housing, Type 'B', for the Aeronautical Technical Center (Centro Técnico de Aeronautica) / 1947 / São José dos Campos, São Pau

In the Type 'B' blocks, as opposed to Type 'A', each unit of a set of eighteen is two stories high.

The living room, which has a higher ceiling, is connected to the bedroom gallery by a staircase of extremely light design and communicates directly with a small garden to one side and the *pilotis* area beneath the bedrooms. Automobiles can be kept in this are which, besides its use as a covered terrace, also shelters the livi room from excess sunshine.

Each dwelling has three bedrooms on the upper floor and a maid room on the ground floor next to the service yard.

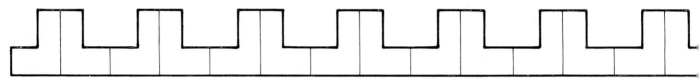

Block plan 1:1000

Section 1:400

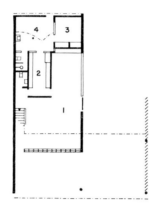

Ground floor 1:400

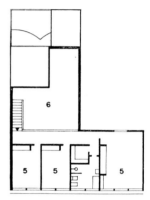

Upper floor 1:400

1 *Living-Dining*
2 *Kitchen*
3 *Maid*
4 *Service yard*
5 *Bedroom*
6 *Upper part of living room*

aff housing, Type 'C-1', for the Aeronautical Technical Center (Centro Técnico de Aeronautica) / 1947 / São José dos Campos, São Paulo

the Type 'C-1' blocks, each with twelve to fourteen dwellings, e layout is similar to that of Type 'B'. The living room, however, ves directly onto the front of the block as well as onto the small

lateral patio, protection from too much sun being provided by wide eaves and *brise-soleil* partly enclosing the front terrace. Next to the maid's room a garage communicates with the lateral patio.

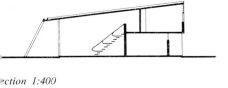

ction 1:400

1 *Living-Dining*
2 *Kitchen*
3 *Maid*
4 *Garage*
5 *Bedroom*

round floor 1:400

Upper floor 1:400

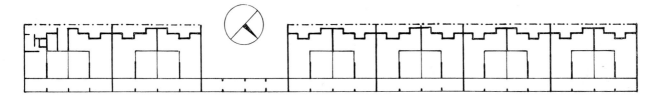

Staff housing, Type 'C-2', for the Aeronautical Technical Center (Centro Técnico de Aeronautica) / 1947 / São José dos Campos, São Paulo

Type 'C-2' is a variation of Type 'C-1' designed for smaller families requiring only two bedrooms. Each block contains twenty housing units, but there are no private garages; there is, however, a shelter where a car can be kept in the private garden in front of each living room. In each of the types illustrated (A, B, C-1 and C-2) one should observe the richness of effect obtained by varying the millwork and *brise-soleil* as well as by the occasional use of exposed brick and openwork walls of different patterns.

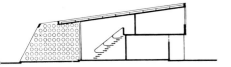

Section 1:400

1 *Living-Dining*
2 *Kitchen*
3 *Maid*
4 *Carport*
5 *Bedroom*
6 *Upper part of living room*

Ground floor 1:400

Upper floor 1:400

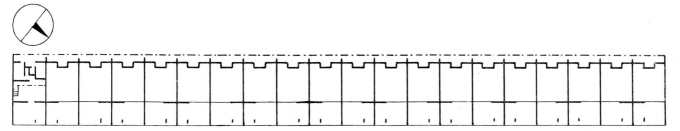

Block plan 1:1000

CARLOS FREDERICO FERREIRA

Housing development for industrial workers / 1949 / Santo André, São Paulo

This low cost development, comprising 594 family apartments for industrial workers, forms part of a wide area of similar housing projects, in which the grade school illustrated on page 134 and designed by the same architect, is also located. The apartments are grouped in three-story blocks raised on *pilotis* with a staircase for each two units. The area underneath the blocks is arranged as a playground with a sandbox in the middle. The laundry sinks in this area are only for emergency use.

This project is typical of the best standard practice prevailing among the social insurance and welfare institutes.

1 Sand-box
2 Laundry tub
3 Living-Dining
4 Bedroom

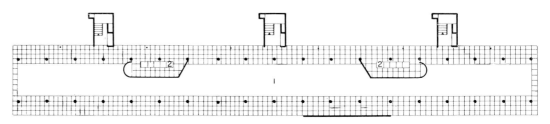

Ground floor 1:400

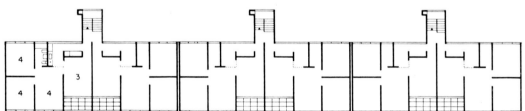

Typical floor 1:400

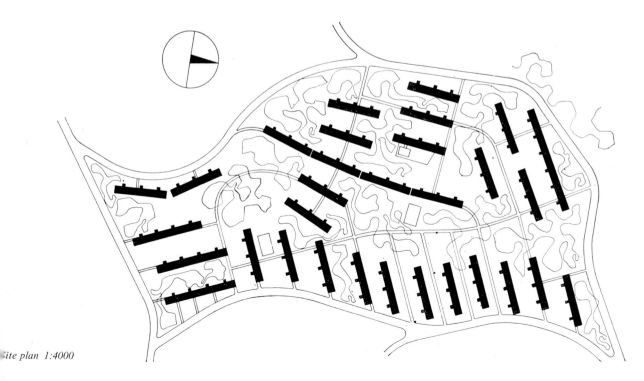

Site plan 1:4000

119

'Pedregulho' housing development, General plan / 1950-52 / Rio de Janeiro

Among the various housing projects envisaged by the City of Rio de Janeiro for low income public employees working in departments near the site, this was the first to be built. The development includes not only the actual housing units, but also all the other essentials from a social point of view: health center, school, sports field, market and laundry. The site, with an area of about 5 hectares (12½ acres), is located on the slopes of Pedregulho Hill in the populous industrial district of São Cristovão. The irregular topography, where differences in level may be as much as 50 meters (164 feet), is offset by the magnificent view to be had from the top of the slope. The project is based on data supplied by the future tenants themselves and checked by personal visits made by the City welfare workers. It is scheduled to hold 478 families of various sizes, housed in single-story studio apartments and duplexes with two to four bedrooms, dimensioned according to the results of the advance census, and arranged in four independent blocks: Block 'A' (272 units), a long seven-story building winding along the hillside (page 122); Blocks 'B-1' and 'B-2' (28 units each) four stories high (page 124); and Block 'C', with twelve floors and 150 apartments, still to be built, all raised on *pilotis*. The general plan provides for a school, with gymnasium and swimmingpool (page 126), a laundry and market (page 128), and a health center (page 129). The nursery and kindergarten, to be annexed to Block 'C', have not yet been built. Communication between the various elements of the development has been kept entirely clear of automobile traffic. Only one street crosses the site and here a small underground passageway provides the people living in Block 'C' with safe access to the main area. Each block is supplied with adequate parking space. The raised form of construction ensures plenty of fresh air reaching every part of the site, gardens and playgrounds.

The units are to be rented only to employees of the City of Rio, and they and their families must submit to a medical examination to show that they are not afflicted with any contagious disease;

furthermore, there is a clause in the lease providing for compulsory periodical inspection by officials of the Workers' Housing Department *(Departamento de Habitação Popular)*. Each tenant will have the right to the free laundering of 2 kilograms (about 4½ lbs.) of washing per week and per person living in the apartment. The cost of this service is included in the rent, excess weight only to be charged separately. The garbage is consigned to main garbage chutes and incinerated. Rentals are deducted from the payroll. The difference between the rentals actually collected from the tenants of the development and those they would have to pay if figured on the basis of a normal return on capital investment amounts in reality to a disguised form of government subsidy. In point of fact, the two major reasons for the scarcity of low-cost housing are the lack of a suitable policy for subsidizing rentals in public housing projects, and demagogic propaganda encouraging the worker to aim at having a house of his own, which funnels many efforts toward the achievement of this end despite the fact that it is beyond the means of the greater part of the population in the large cities. However, it is not merely in a social sense or from the point of view of workers' housing technique that the Pedregulho development stands out among its fellows. It is at the same time an architectural achievement of the highest order revealing in the plastic arrangement of the various elements, in the treatment applied to the elevations, which is esthetically sound as well as functional, and in the work of the artists who collaborated with the architect (Portinari, Burle Marx, Anísio Medeiros), all the differences between Brazilian architecture and the international architecture from which it stems. These differences are equally striking in the Niemeyer development (pages 112–117) and in that designed by Bolonha (pages 130–132); despite limitations set by an inadequate legal and financial framework, they can also be traced in the execution of the Carlos Ferreira project (pages 118–119).

1 Water reservoir
2 Apartment block 'A'
3 Apartment block 'B1'
4 Apartment block 'B2'
5 Apartment block 'C'
6 Primary school
7 Gymnasium
8 Lockers
9 Swimming pool
10 Basket ball
11 Wading pool
12 Playground
13 Health center
14 Laundry
15 Market
16 Day nursery
17 Nursery school
18 Kindergarten
19 Underground passage for pedestrians
20 Pre-existing workshop

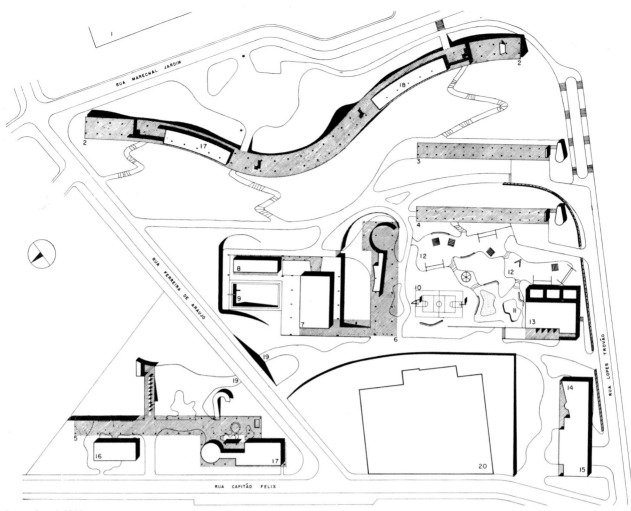

General site plan 1:2000

AFFONSO EDUARDO REIDY

'Pedregulho' housing development, Apartment block 'A' / 1950-52 / Rio de Janeiro

This block is on the way to completion; 260 meters (about 850 feet) in length, following the winding contours of the hillside, it recalls in its general outline Le Corbusier's early projects for Algiers, dating from 1931. The third story, free for the most part of dividing walls so as to form a covered playground, contains the administrative offices, social services, nursery and kindergarten while at the far end there is an acoustic shell for a children theater. Below are two stories of single-room apartments, leaving the four upper stories for two series of duplexes with two bedrooms each. Three main staircases provide access to the various floors.

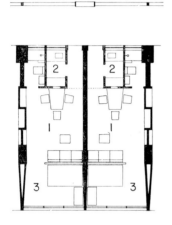

Plan of one-room apartments 1:200

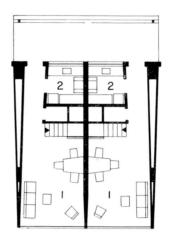

Plan of duplex apartments, lower floor 1:200

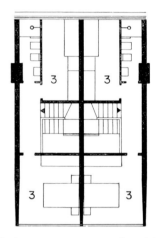

Plan of duplex apartments, upper floor 1:200

1 Living-Dining
2 Kitchen
3 Bedroom

Main stairway
Circulation
Living-Dining
Bedroom

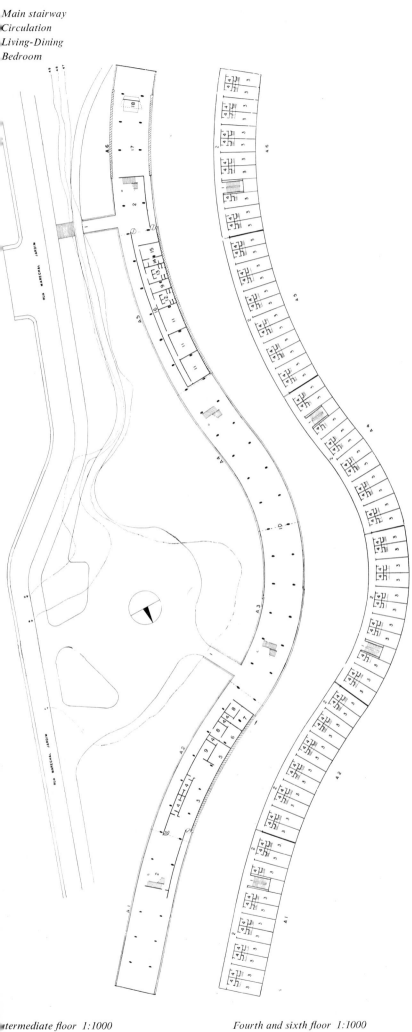

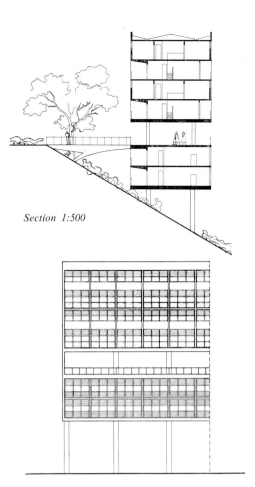

Section 1:500

Partial front elevation 1:500

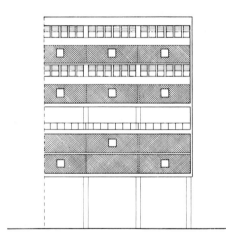

Partial rear elevation 1:500

Intermediate floor 1:1000

Fourth and sixth floor 1:1000

1 Bridge
2 Hall
3 Game room
4 Toilets
5 Teachers' room
6 Social workers
7 Superintendent
8 Waiting
9 Cot storage
10 Lounge
11 Playroom
12 Boys' W.C.
13 Girls' W.C.
14 Teachers' W.C.
15 Administration
16 Gallery
17 Children's theater
18 Acoustic shell

AFFONSO EDUARDO REIDY

'Pedregulho' housing development, Apartment blocks 'B-1' and 'B-2' / 1950-52 / Rio de Janeiro

In the type 'B' blocks, which have four stories on *pilotis*, the compact ingenious plan of each unit is so arranged that one of the three standard rooms can be annexed to the neighboring unit to form one two-room and one four-room apartment. Thus, while Block 'A' only caters to single persons, childless couples or small families, 'B' blocks can accomodate small, medium and large families. The verandas of each unit are protected partly by balustrades and partly by openwork concrete screens alternating in the upper and lower series to produce an attractive pattern on the façade and clearly expressing the two-story design of the duplex apartments.

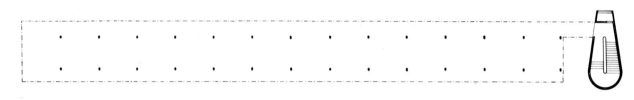

Ground floor 1:500

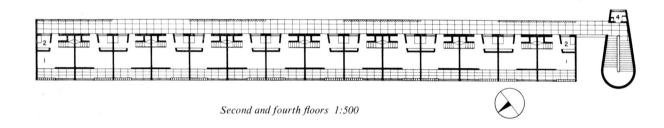

Second and fourth floors 1:500

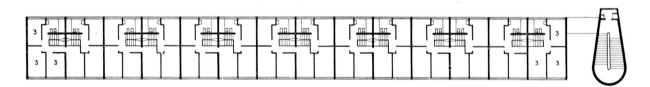

1 Kitchen
2 Living-Dining
3 Bedroom

Third and fifth floors 1:500

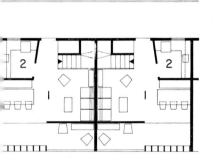

ower floor of typical duplex apartment 1:200   *Upper floor 1:200*   *Alternate upper floor 1:200*

AFFONSO EDUARDO REIDY

'Pedregulho' housing development, Primary school and gymnasium / 1950-52 / Rio de Janeiro

With the gymnasium and swimming pool, the school forms a well-balanced composition. In a single block raised on *pilotis* and reached by a wide covered ramp, it contains five classrooms holding 40 children each (7 to 11 years of age). The classrooms have a southern exposure and open onto covered terraces of generous dimensions, which can also be used for classwork on hot days. Cross ventilation is obtained by openings in the wall of the corridor, which is enclosed on the outer side only by an openwork screen of hollow tile blocks. In addition to the classrooms, there are a library, a lounge, administrative offices, locker rooms and toilets on the top floor. In the *pilotis* area under the building, used as a covered playground, a canteen, small kitchen and toilets are included; a mosaic mural by Burle Marx adds a pleasing touch. The striking *azulejo* panel in the gymnasium block is the work of Portinari.

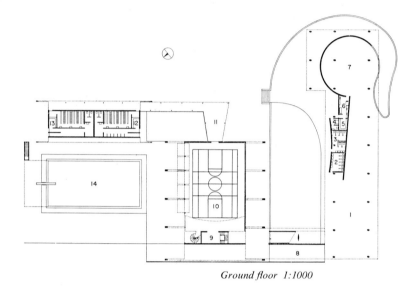

Ground floor 1:1000

1 Hall and administration
2 Terrace
3 Principal and Secretary
4 Secretary's W.C.
5 Principal's W.C.
6 Library
7 Classroom
8 Teachers' W.C.
9 Girls' W.C.
10 Boys' W.C.
11 Corridor
12 Ramp
13 Balcony
14 Gymnasium
15 Shelter
16 Roof of lockers

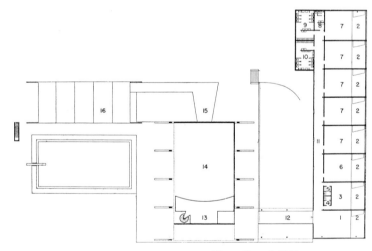

Upper floor 1:1000

Covered recreation area
Boys' W.C.
Girls' W.C.
Service W.C.
Food storage
Kitchen
Lunch room
Ramp
Storage
Gymnasium
Shelter
Boys' lockers
Girls' lockers
Swimming pool

AFFONSO EDUARDO REIDY

'Pedregulho' housing development, Laundry and market / 1950 / Rio de Janeiro

The market and the laundry, essential to the efficient servicing of the development, are housed in one building located near the street bordering the site, with a service entrance and parking space for loading and unloading delivery trucks. The roof slopes down towards the center where it is lowered to form a wide trough running the whole length of the building with the object of providing cross ventilation in all the rooms. A movable horizontal *brise-soleil*, partially protecting the side where the public enters, corresponds to the central part of the market. The latter has boxes for dry goods, meat, fish, groceries and dairy produce; cold storage and refrigerated counters are provided. There is also a bakery with an electric oven.

The machine laundry is mechanical and operated by skill workers; separate sections deal with reception, marking, disinfe tion, washing, drying, ironing, storing and delivery.

Despite some initial prejudice motivated by tenants' reluctance display clothes in bad condition, the central laundry has prov to be one of the most valuable adjuncts to the developmen Apart from the availability in every plan of extra space usual reserved for the laundry sink, the advantage for the housewi is that she has more time for housework; furthermore, it mak it easy for every tenant to wear clothes that are well washed a ironed.

1 Customers
2 Grocery shop
3 Butcher
4 Fish
5 Vegetables and fruit
6 Dairy products
7 Bakery shop
8 Cold storage
9 Groceries (storage)
10 Bakery
11 Women's W.C.
12 Men's W.C.

13 Flour (storage)
14 Gallery
15 Service entrance
16 Reception
17 Management
18 Delivery
19 Boilers
20 Laundry
21 Ready laundry
22 Women's W.C.
23 Men's W.C.

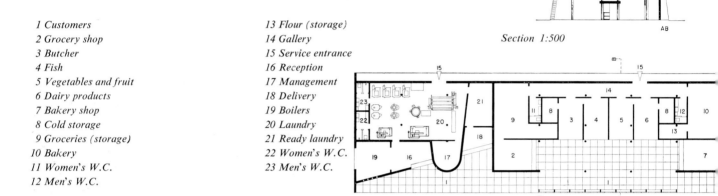

Section 1:500

Plan 1:500

The health center, located in another independent pavilion, is designed to cope with preventive care, medical consultation and dental work, as well as emergency cases and minor surgical operations.

The program includes: a registry and office for classifying patients; three doctor's consulting rooms; one dentist's consulting room, with a laboratory and dark room; a pharmacy; a surgery for minor operations, and annexes; a small analytical laboratory; three wards for men, women and children respectively, together with the indispensable workrooms. The wards are intended for rest purposes and for accomodating in-patients over short periods.

The waiting room, partly outdoors, is lined on one side by a long concrete bench, fitting well into the layout, and on the other by a mural in *azulejos* designed by Anísio Medeiros.

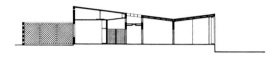

Section 1:500

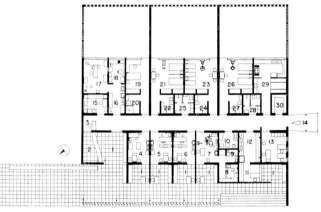
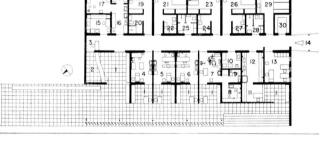

Plan 1:500

Hall
Registration
Nurse's station
Preventive care (children)
Preventive care (women)
Preventive care (men)
Dentist
Dental laboratory
Dark room
Utility room
Pharmacy
Pharmacy workroom
Management
Employees' entrance
Laboratory
Scrub-up
Operating
Sterilizing
Doctors
Doctors' W.C.
Women's ward
Women's W.C.
Children's ward
Children's W.C.
Male nurses' W.C.
Men's ward
Men's W.C.
Nurses' W.C.
Dining and kitchen
Linen

FRANCISCO BOLONHA

'Paquetá' housing project / 1952 / Paquetá, Rio de Janeiro

Like the Pedregulho project, this small group of 27 dwellings built on an island in Guanabara Bay is intended for the lower grades of City employees working in general services and utilities in zones near the site—in this particular case, street-cleaners, who earn the lowest wages of all. Here again the rentals paid are but a fraction of what they would be were it not for the disguised subsidy furnished by the City.

The outside corridors leading to the dwellings overlook a garden where there is a playground and a basketball court. On the other side stands the watchman's lodge and a small pavilion for management and social work.

Though it was begun after Pedregulho, the project is so much smaller that is was finished earlier.

The two blocks, one with 16 and the other with 11 units, have been laid out in such a way as not to interfere with the luxuriant vegetation that is an attractive feature of the numerous islands scattered over the bay.

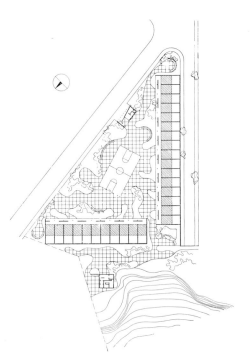

General site plan 1:2000

Each dwelling has a small patio connected to the high-ceilinged living room and enclosed on the outer side (falling away from the playground) by an openwork brick wall. The ground floor also contains a dining nook, a kitchen and a small terrace for the laundry sink. On the upper floor there are two bedrooms and a bathroom. The staircase and the bathroom are lighted by a clerestory above the living room roof. The corridors on the play-ground side are screened in front of the entrance doors and dining nooks by hollow tile panels. The bedroom windows are of the horizontal sliding sash type, and permanent ventilation is provided all along the top of the wall above them.

In the watchman's lodge there is a mural in cement tile by Anísio Medeiros.

Section 1:400

Ground floor 1:200

Upper floor of one unit 1:200

1 Living
2 Kitchen
3 Bedroom

Schools, Hospitals

Religious buildings, Sports and Recreation

Museums and Exhibition buildings

CARLOS FREDERICO FERREIRA

Primary school / 1949 / Santo André, São Paulo

This school with a capacity for 1,206 pupils in two shifts serves the neighborhood in which the housing project illustrated on page 118 and designed by the same architect is situated. The rational, straightforward solution adopted in the layout consists in linking the two classroom blocks by covered passageways. The program also called for an independent water-tower, and the quiet dignity of its design stresses the social purpose and functional character of the project.

The classrooms, oriented so as to receive as little sun as possible in summer and yet to be sunny enough in winter, are built over the *pilotis* area forming the covered playground under each block.

The administration offices are in the first of these playgrounds and

a small farming club in the second. In the gymnasium there is small canteen. Access from one floor to the next is obtained by t use of ramps throughout. The outer wall of the classrooms is glaz from top to bottom; the lower part of the frame is fixed but t upper part carries a swivel sash so that cross ventilation can established with the communication gallery.

The elevations clearly show the economical way in which t problem has been solved. The fenestration of the long horizont façades, reduced to the simple expression of structural membe and framing, gains originality of proportion from the lintel sep rating the lower, fixed half of each frame from the movable upp part.

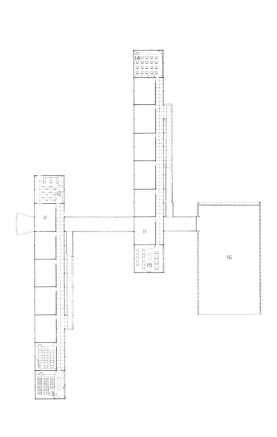

Upper floor 1:1000

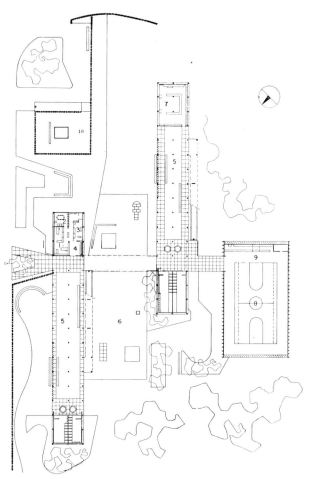

Ground floor 1:1000

1 *Secretary*
2 *Teachers' room*
3 *Doctors and dentists*
4 *Waiting room*
5 *Recreation shelter*
6 *Patio*
7 *Farming club*
8 *Gymnasium*
9 *Children's canteen*
10 *Water tower*
11 *Classroom*
12 *Library and geography classroom*
13 *Physics and natural sciences*
14 *Drawing and map-making*
15 *Manual training*
16 *Upper part of gymnasium*

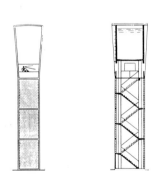

Water tower elevation and section 1:400

FRANCISCO BOLONHA

Kindergarten / 1952 / Vitória, Espirito Santo

By building this kindergarten in one corner of a city block with an area of about 26,500 meters (over $6^1/_2$ acres) the architect left the greater part of the site available for a park and playground of generous proportions. In the landscaping, full advantage has been taken of an existing pond, and its serpentine shape, with many a meander and leafy islet, enhances the picturesque setting. Facing the main building on the other side of the garden, an acoustic shell of reinforced concrete covers the stage of a little outdoor theater with tiers formed by concentric concrete strips.

The classrooms open onto small patios which can be used for working out-of-doors. They are five in number, but the proje also includes a music room, a rest room and a refectory.

The care taken over the formal aspect of the design, evidenced the mural in vitrified mosaic tile by Anísio Medeiros (covering t wall on the street side of the court) has in no way impaired t functional efficiency of the layout.

Actually the building is tucked away unpretentiously amid t vegetation of the park, and the unconventional arrangement of t planted and paved areas checks any tendency towards institutior rigidity that might dampen the carefree gaiety of the children they play beneath the shady trees.

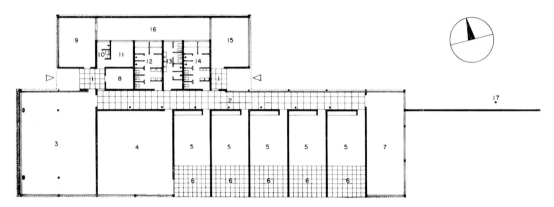

Plan of Kindergarten 1:500

1 Entrance
2 Gallery
3 Lunchroom
4 Restroom
5 Classroom
6 Patio
7 Music room
8 Storage
9 Kitchen
10 Watchman's W.C.
11 Watchman
12 Girls' W.C.
13 Teachers' W.C.
14 Boys' W.C.
15 Secretary
16 Service yard
17 Flag pole

General plan 1:2000
A Kindergarten
B Outdoor theater

EDUARDO CORONA

Penha State College / 1952 / São Paulo

The slope of the two-corner lot on which this school is located made it necessary to lay out the building on three levels, of which only the intermediate one covers the area of the site.

On the first level, not excavated under the auditorium, the *pilotis* area (except where it is taken up by the dressing-rooms of the swimming pool, the student club office, the medical service and the janitor's apartment) provides a covered playground in connection with the garden. On the second level are to be found the administration offices, a small library, classrooms, handicraft workshops, and the auditorium. On the third level, restricted to the part above the classrooms on the floor below, additional class rooms, laboratories and an amphitheater are located. The thr levels are connected by staircases and ramps.

By the use of *pilotis*, the architect has succeeded in compensati to some extent for the inadequacy of the site so as to produce a attractive design.

It need hardly be pointed out that the unfortunate little gard wall was an afterthought; it provides just another instance of th lack of understanding which so often arises between the artist a the bureaucrat.

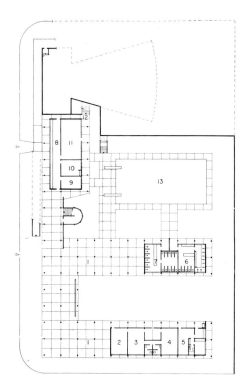

Lower floor 1:1000

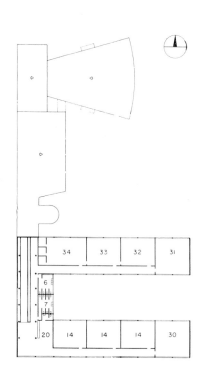

Main floor 1:1000

Upper floor 1:1000

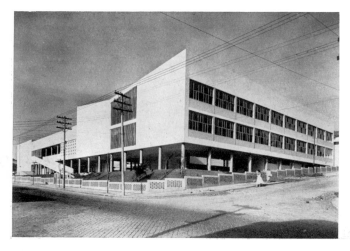

This school in the capital of the state of Rio de Janeiro, across the bay from the Federal capital, and that illustrated on the following pages and located in São Paulo, are good examples of the work of the National Service of Industrial Apprenticeship, abbreviated, in Portuguese, to s.e.n.a.i.

This self-governing agency, organized and supported by Management, in the form of a contribution of $1^0/_0$ of the pay-roll of every industrial concern in the country, was founded in 1942 and provides vocational training for apprentices from 14 to 18 years of age, already working in industrial plants. It now gives instruction in about 80 different trades and has 107 schools in various parts of the country, in which more than 30 000 students are enrolled.

Apart from its basic courses and scholarships awarded to its own technicians and professors for post-graduate studies abroad, the s.e.n.a.i. runs nightschools for the vocational training of adults in beginners' and refresher courses, and industrial technical schools

with pilot plants, for training skilled personnel such as foremen master craftsmen and industrial technicians.

The Niterói school turns out mechanics in a number of branches and carpenters, ships' carpenters and joiners, with a total enrolment of 480 at the present time.

The project was subject to two main conditions: the extreme irregularity of the site, which was, moreover, very small for the program, and the fact that the measurements of the workshop pavilion were predetermined, use being made of a wartime aircraft hangar, imported from England. This is why the workshops were located on the broadest part of the site, next to the truck entrance. In the remaining inner area, three blocks of classrooms are set slightly askew to obtain better orientation, and connected up by a marquese to the other parts of the project. In front, the only building with a façade on the street, houses the Administration offices and Students' Entrance, with the Library, Storeroom and Medical Service on the mezzanine.

1 Students' entrance
2 Trucks
3 Drafting room
4 Classroom
5 Sports
6 Foundry
7 Workshop
8 Metal work
9 Secretary
10 Lounge
11 Teachers' room
12 Library
13 Veranda
14 Doctor's office

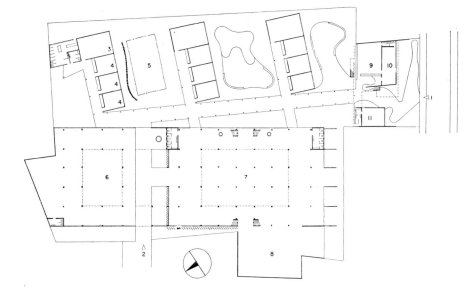

Mezzanine 1:1000

Plan 1:1000

HELIO QUEIROZ DUARTE and E. R. DE CARVALHO MANGE

'Anchieta' school for industrial apprentices / 1954 / São Paulo

The sense of progressive experimentation that should distinguish school architecture of today, even more in interpreting the program than in formal research, and which has been observed in the preceding examples, is clearly expressed in the planning of this vocational school which has an enrollment of 140 students and a similar curriculum to that of the one on page 140. The fusion of theory and practice, which is fundamental in the teaching methods adopted by the SENAI is carried out on the architectural plane by integrating the classrooms with the general layout of the workshops and the garden courtyard by means of the circulation gallery that forms a part of the shops and provides access to the various bays, and of the footbridges thrown across the patio to connect this gallery with the classrooms. It is also part of the SENAI's policy of educating the public to let the man in the street see as much as possible of what goes on in the school; this is essential in a country that lies in urgent need of rapid and sufficient industrialization. In addition to the school workshops, the program called for classrooms, and offices for the management, as well as for medical and dental care (located under the classrooms); in a separate building, an auditorium, assembly hall and library; and finally a sports ground with swimming pool.

The use of movable storage walls between classrooms enables the latter to be adjusted in size to take care of changing requirements. The composition is completed by a statue of Anchieta, the great teaching missionary of early colonial times and patron of the school, by the sculptor G. Fraccaroli.

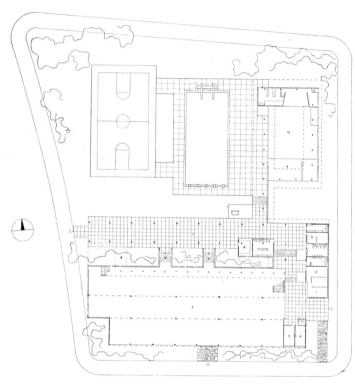

Lower floor 1:1000

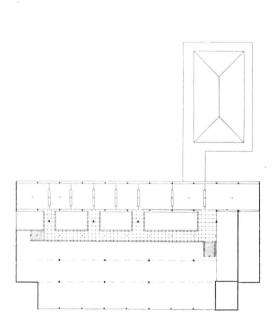

Upper floor 1:1000

1 *Secretary*
2 *Director*
3 *Social worker*
4 *Dentist*
5 *Doctor*
6 *Shop*
7 *Recreation and dining room*
8 *Pantry*
9 *Library*
10 *Recreation hall*
11 *Classroom*

142

OSCAR NIEMEYER

'Obra do Berço' day nursery / 1937 / Rio de Janeiro

The first building completed by Oscar Niemeyer was this day nursery which dispenses medical advice and assistance to expectant and nursing mothers, and assistance to children up to two years of age, besides maintaining a free service of milk distribution. The front block is four stories high and the rear block two, surmounted by a roof garden. The fourth floor, front, consists of one large multiple-use room, divided by movable partitions.

There is an interesting story attached to the *brise-soleil* on the main façade. These were originally intended to be fixed and made up of hollow concrete elements similar to those used in the Brazilian Pavilion at the New York World's Fair (page 180), the horizon-

tal slabs being tilted forwards so as to secure better shelter fro[m] the afternoon sun. The work was carried out in the architect['s] absence and failure to follow the detail drawing resulted in th[e] slabs being set in such a way that they could not provide the r[e]quired protection. In order to satisfy the well-founded claims [of] the institution owning the building and to avoid damaging th[e] incipient, if growing, prestige of modern Brazilian architectur[e] Niemeyer replaced the whole set on the main façade at his ow[n] cost, using the present system of adjustable vertical slabs, inspire[d] by the design of the Brazilian Press Association building (page 194[)] in which the *brise-soleil* were, however, fixed.

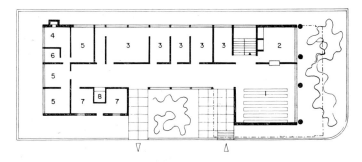

Ground floor 1:400

1 Waiting room
2 Secretary
3 Consultations
4 Kitchen
5 Employees
6 Bath
7 Preparation of milk
8 Distribution of milk
9 Sewing room
10 Infants' nursery
11 Director
12 Storage
13 Nurse
14 Isolation ward
15 Dining room
16 Lounge

Second floor 1:400

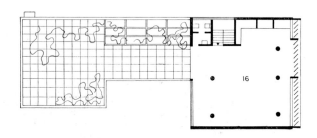

Third floor 1:400

FRANCISCO BOLONHA

Maternity hospital / 1951 / Cataguázes, Minas Gerais

This small maternity and children's hospital was built as part of a much larger hospital project in a small town in the state of Minas Gerais. This town poses a typical Brazilian paradox, for although it has a population of only 20 000, it can boast a large number of modern buildings, including, among others, private houses by Aldary Toledo (page 28), Francisco Bolonha, Edgard Guimarães do Vale, and Oscar Niemeyer, a hotel by Aldary Toledo and Gilberto Lyra de Lemos, and a school by Oscar Niemeyer.

The building has only one floor and is designed in the form of a long block with the obstetrical department to the extreme right;

at the other end are the kitchen and offices, laundry and pharmacy the entrance hall is west center and on the east side there are t children's wards and covered playground. The formal treatme of the plan is softened, in the elevations, by the use of gay and u pretentious details that lend the building an almost resident character. To give greater plastic unity to the design, the slidi doors in the covered playground repeat in wooden trellis work t scale and pattern of the hollow tile blocks used in the lar screen panel.

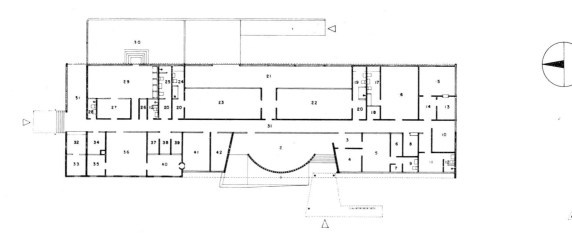

Plan 1:500

ESCRITÓRIO TÉCNICO DA CIDADE UNIVERSITÁRIA DA UNIVERSIDADE DO BRASIL, *Technical Offi* *of the University City - University of Brazil* **Jorge Machado Moreira**, *Chief architect*, **Aldary Henriques Toledo**, *Assistant architect*

Orlando Magdalena, João Henrique Rocha, Donato Mello Junior, Giuseppina Pirro, Adele Weber, Renato Ferreira de Sá, Elias Kaufma **Arlindo Araujo Gomes, João Corrêa Lima, Asthor Read Sá Roris, Norma Cavalcanti de Albuquerque, Otavio Sergio de Moraes, Carl** **Alberto Boudet Fernandes, Conceição M. Mattos Penna, Jorge Werneck Passos, Paulo Rocha Souza, Renato Sá Junior** *and* **Paulo Porciúncu** **de Sá** *collaborating architects*

Institute of Child Welfare (University of Brazil) 'Instituto de Puericultura' / 1953 / Rio de Janeiro

The Institute of Child Welfare, which earned an award in the hospital class of the Second Biennial Exhibition of São Paulo (1953), was designed and built under the direction of the *Escritório Técnico da Cidade Universitária do Brasil*, headed by Engineer L. H. Horta Barbosa.

The sobriety of its conception, coupled with the disciplined ingenuity which presides over the development of the project, as much in the general design as in the slightest details, is an indication of the real profound classicism of the work as a whole, which will certainly prove to be one of the landmarks of modern architecture in Brazil.

The lightness of the large blocks, with their clean-cut outline, raise on *pilotis*, and treatment contrasting wide expanses of smoo surfaces with the tracery of ceramic tilework and with glazed ti murals (designed by Roberto Burle Marx, Aylton Sá Rêgo, ar Yvanildo da Silva Gusmão), no less than the detail peculiar each part and the spreading gardens landscaped by Roberto Bur Marx, stresses the distinctly regional character of this work.

The Institute of Child Welfare, which was the first building to completed of the University City still under construction (page 23 covers a total area of 16 074 square meters (173 000 square fe or close on four acres) of floor space to be devoted to studie

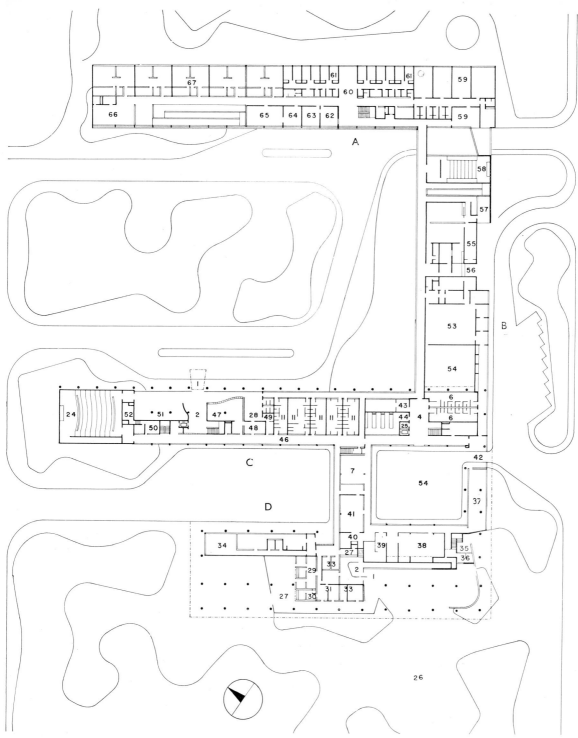

Plan at second level 1:1000

A Nursery second floor
B Milk bank ground floor
C Hospital ground floor
D Out-patients dept. ground floor

 1 Main entrance
 2 Main hall
 3 Information
 4 Service hall
 5 Employees' entrance
 6 Employees' lockers
 7 Employees' dining room
 8 Serving area
 9 Staff dining room
10 Lounge
11 Staff's lockers
12 Filter
13 Nurse's station
14 Children's toilet

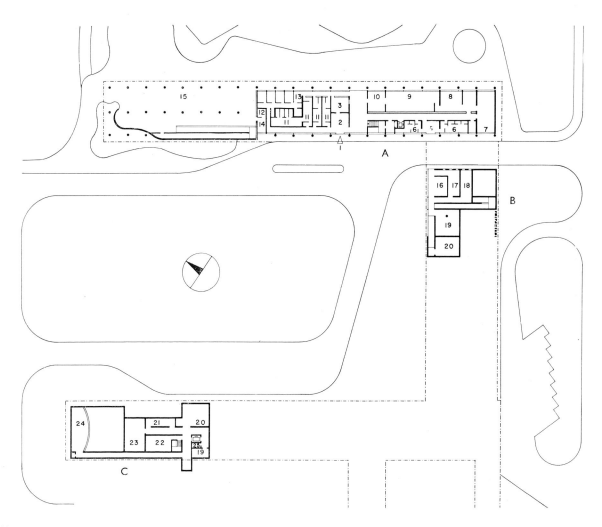

Plan at lower level 1:1000

15 Playground
16 Garbage cans, soiled
17 Garbage cans, clean
18 Can washing
19 Boiler room
20 Power plant
21 Electrician's shop
22 Record storage
23 Air conditioning
24 Lecture room
25 Elevator machine room
16 Garden
17 Information
18 Waiting room
19 Social service
20 Medical records
21 Admission and registration
22 Public toilets
23 Doctors' toilets
24 Pathology
25 Suspect anteroom
26 Canteen
27 Food storage
28 General kitchen
29 Serving area
30 Formula room
31 Formula room
32 Service entrance
33 Linen
34 General storage
35 Soiled circulation
36 Clean circulation
37 Administrative office
38 Administrator's office
39 Admitting office

A Nursery ground floor
B Milk bank basement
C Hospital basement

research and teaching of a biological and social nature with reference to the physical and mental development of the child. Located in the Medical Sector and on the outskirts of the University City in order to make it easier of access for out-patients, it stands next to the Clinics Hospital and the future Maternity Hospital, and consists of four blocks: *a*. Out-patients' Department; *b*. Hospital; *c*. Child Study Department; *d*. Milk Bank.

The Out-patients' Department, with two stories, and a part raised on *pilotis*, covers an area of some 4 000 meters (about 43 000 square feet) of floor space. Its normal capacity is about 200 children in each shift. Social Service, Consulting Rooms for Preliminary Diagnosis and General Services are located on the ground floor. After classification, contagious patients will be isolated from the non-contagious and sent by separate means of access to the second floor, which is divided into the following consulting rooms: Child Care, Clinical Pediatrics (for infants only), Cardiology, Nose and Throat, Ophthalmology, Dentistry, Psychology and Neuro-psychiatry, Physiodiagnostics and Physiotherapy, Bio

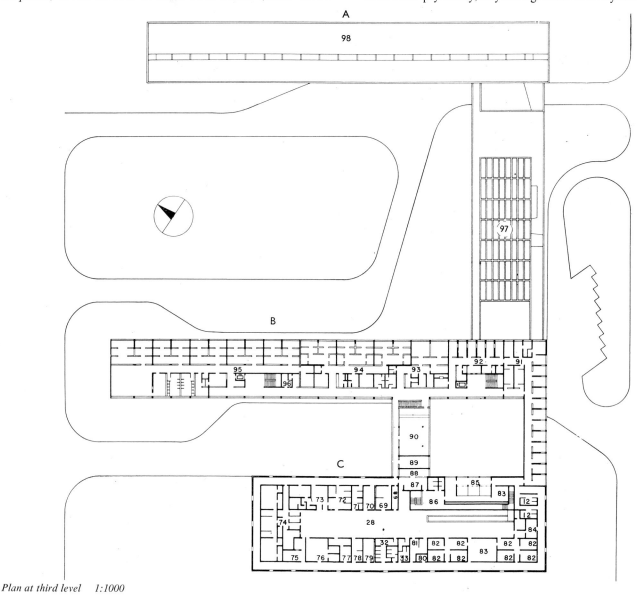

Plan at third level   1:1000

A Nursery roof
B Hospital second floor
C Out-patients dept. second floor

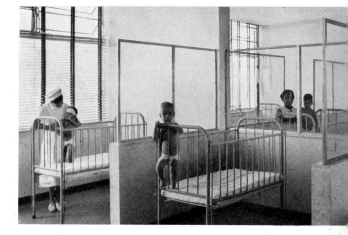

hetrics, Basal Metabolism, Allergy, X-ray and Analytical Laboratories. A Laboratory of Pathological Anatomy is also installed
in this block to attend to the hospital requirements and also to
accept outside work. On the ground floor there is a food canteen
for children; one counter is in the entrance lobby, while the other
is in the exit lobby for infectious patients.

The Hospital has three stories with a total capacity of 107 beds
and covers an area of 7 222 square meters (77 500 square feet) of
floor space. The 107 beds are distributed among five wards as
follows: Observation, 6; Premature births, 16; Nursing mothers,
24; Children from 2 to 7 years of age, 50 Isolation, 11. The Child
Study Department has a two-floor building of its own covering
an area of 3 490 square meters (37 500 square feet) and is mainly
intended for admitting 84 healthy children, 12 of them accompanied by their nursing mothers, for studies in child dietetics and
development.

The Hospital is connected with the Child Study Department by
1 356 square meters (14 600 square feet) of floor space, including
the Mothers' Milk Bank, pens for keeping experimental animals
and miscellaneous services.

60 Photography
61 Museum
62 Projection booth
63 Animal quarters
64 Yard
65 Milk bank
66 Milk bank, sales
67 Blood donors' hall
68 Classroom
69 Nurses' lodgings
60 Mothers' rest room
61 Mothers and infants
62 Administration
63 Doctors
64 Pantry

65 Children's dining room
66 Children's lounge
67 Nursery
68 Utility room
69 Cardiology
70 Biometrics
71 Allergy
72 Physical therapy
73 X-ray
74 Laboratory
75 Neuro-psychiatry
76 Nose and throat
77 Ophthalmology
78 Dental suite
79 Records

80 Employees' toilet
81 Injection room
82 Examination room
83 Classroom
84 Treatment
85 Contagious unit, examination
86 Contagious unit, waiting
87 Pharmacy
88 Laboratory
89 Sterilizing
90 Doctors' dining room
91 Contagious room
92 Isolation room
93 Premature ward
94 Nursery

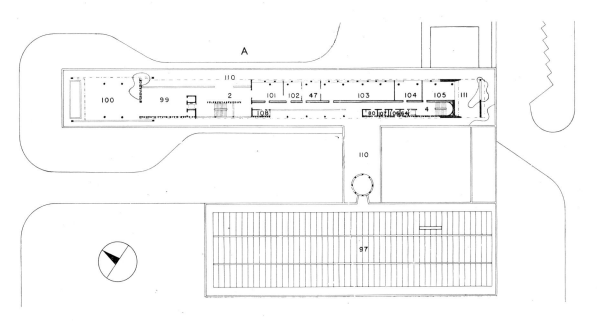

Plan at fourth level   1:1000
Hospital third floor

95 Children's ward (2 to 7)
96 Doctors' room
97 Shed
98 Roof
99 Playroom
100 Covered recreation
101 Conference room
102 Professor's room
103 Library and files
104 Research
105 Staff lounge
106 Women's toilet
107 Men's toilet
108 Doctor's toilet
109 Nurse's toilet
110 Terrace
111 Pergola

Tenth, eleventh and twelfth floors 1:500

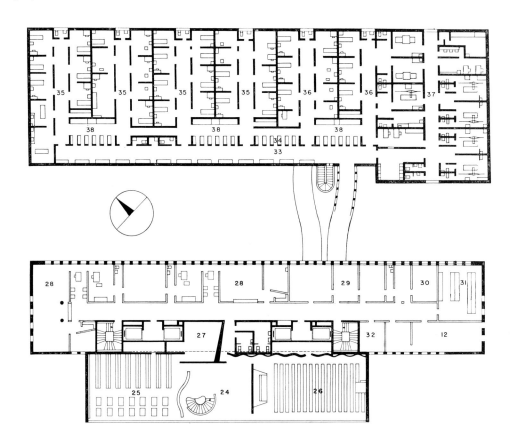

Fifth floor 1:500

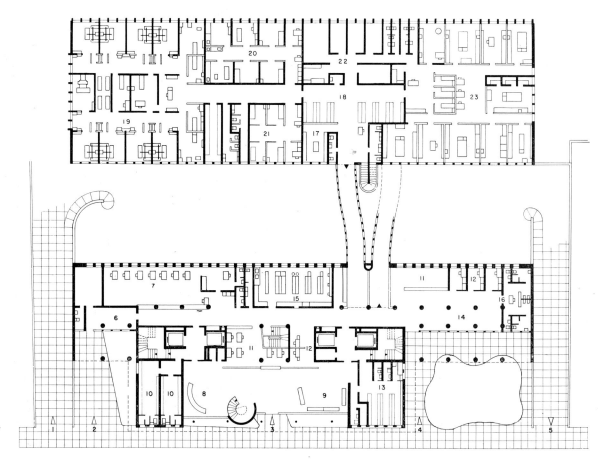

Fourth floor
1:500

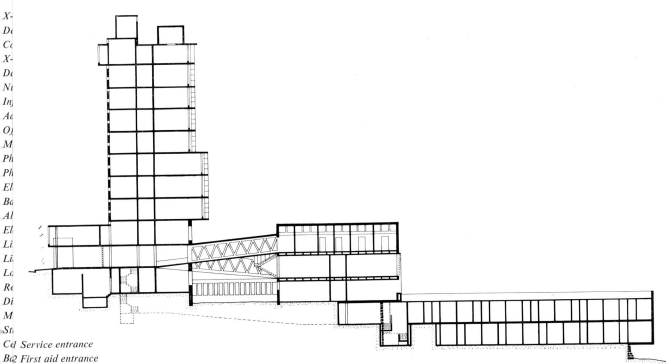

Section 1:500

1 Service entrance
2 First aid entrance
3 Patients', doctors', nurses' and public entrance
4 Out-patients' entrance
5 Funerals
6 First aid
7 Business office
8 Waiting room for paying patients
9 Waiting room for non-paying patients
0 Doctors' and nurses' lockers
1 Admittance and cashier
2 Social service
3 Non-paying patients' dressing and bathrooms
4 Out-patients' waiting room
5 Pharmacy
6 Non-paying out-patients' bath
7 Waiting room for paying out-patients
8 Waiting room for non-paying out-patient
9 X-ray therapy
0 Radium
1 Electro-therapy
2 Photography
3 Laboratories
4 Lobby
5 Library
6 Auditorium
7 Museum of anatomy and pathology
8 Headquarters of the Cancer Association
9 Hospital director
0 Chief nurse
1 Technical files
2 Dietician
3 Waiting
4 Dressing booths
5 Non-paying out-patients' examination
6 Preventive medicine center
7 X-ray therapy
8 Nurses' station
9 Private room
0 Stretchers
1 Janitor closet
2 Pantry
3 Linen
4 Head nurse
5 Soiled linen
6 Treatment
7 Internes' rest room

OSCAR NIEMEYER

Church of St. Francis / 1943 / Pampulha, Minas Gerais

Situated at the edge of the lake on the banks of which Niemeyer also planned a sports and recreation club (pages 166 to 171), this little church with its novel structural shapes, adapted to the technical possibilities of reinforced concrete, illustrates the urge for constant plastic research that distinguishes this artist and enables him to depart successfully from the more Cartesian conventions of modern architecture.

The nave is parabolic in section and decreases in rise from the front to the altar. On the inside it is faced with wood and on the outside with glazed mosaic tile in a composition by Paulo Werneck. The altar is roofed by another parabola, meeting three other parabolas, one on one side and two on the other, which contain the sacristy and other annexes. The altar is lighted by a clerestory above the parabola of the nave. The front, protected by a *brise-soleil* at the top, is connected by the sloping marquee to the bell-tower, dramatic outline of which contrasts with the curves that domin. the design. The tile mural on the rear façade, depicting the life Saint Francis of Assisi, brother of all creatures, is by Portin who also painted the great altar fresco in which Christ is rep sented as the friend of the sick, the poor and the sinners, and stations of the Cross, hung along either side of the nave.

The construction of this church set off a storm of discussion, a for this reason it was never consecrated by the ecclesiastical thorities. This opposition, which obliged the SPHAN to t charge of the building (on the grounds that it really was a natio monument) seems even more extraordinary in our days, consid ing that a great International Eucharistic Congress was held in de Janeiro before the modern altar shown on page 164.

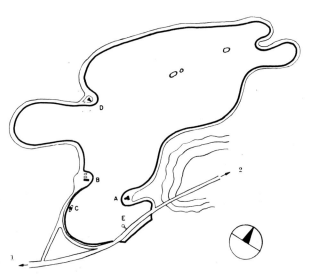

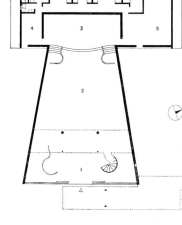

A Casino
B Yacht club
C Restaurant and dance hall
D Church
E Pier
1 To Belo Horizonte
2 To airport (*Lagôa Santa*)

Pampulha lake

Plan of church 1:500

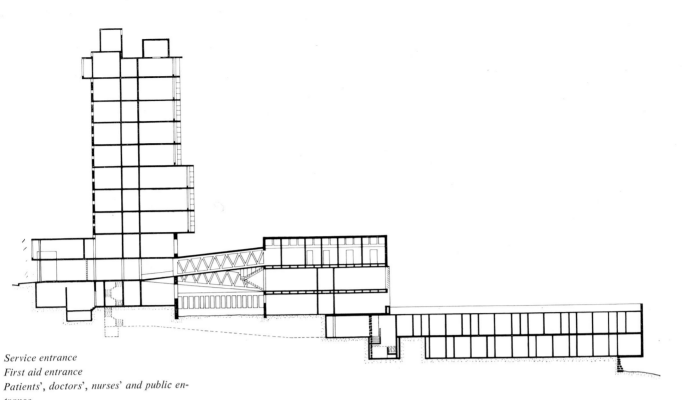

Service entrance
First aid entrance
Patients', doctors', nurses' and public entrance
Out-patients' entrance
Funerals
First aid
Business office
Waiting room for paying patients
Waiting room for non-paying patients
Doctors' and nurses' lockers
Admittance and cashier
Social service
Non-paying patients' dressing and bathrooms
Out-patients' waiting room
Pharmacy
Non-paying out-patients' bath
Waiting room for paying out-patients
Waiting room for non-paying out-patient
X-ray therapy
Radium
Electro-therapy
Photography
Laboratories
Lobby
Library
Auditorium
Museum of anatomy and pathology
Headquarters of the Cancer Association
Hospital director
Chief nurse
Technical files
Dietician
Waiting
Dressing booths
Non-paying out-patients' examination
Preventive medicine center
X-ray therapy
Nurses' station
Private room
Stretchers
Janitor closet
Pantry
Linen
Head nurse
Soiled linen
Treatment
Internes' rest room

Section 1:500

FIRMINO F. SALDANHA

Hospital for Maritime Workers / 1955 / Rio de Janeiro

In this project of a general hospital with 450 beds, for the *Instituto de Assistência Social aos Marítimos* (Maritime Workers' Social Security Institute), the many divergent elements of the program have been integrated into a volume that is both well proportioned and extremely simple. The building has twelve stories above the 'plateau' leading up to the main entrance, and, following the slope of the site, two below this level. The latter two stories and that on a level with the main entrance are assigned to general services,

technical and scientific services, etc. The mezzanine connecting entrance level to the upper floors houses the administrative vices, laboratories, etc. The wards are situated on the next ei floors (2nd to 9th), with a maternity ward on the 10th. The surg division on the 11th floor includes four operating rooms a annexes, while the nurses' living quarters are installed on the 1 floor, next to the solarium and the roof garden, only part of wh is under cover.

Mezzanine 1:500

1 Main entrance
2 Main lobby
3 Patients' hall
4 Patients' elevator
5 Doctors' and public elevator
6 Service elevator
7 Garbage
8 Service hall
9 Soiled linen chute

10 Linen dumbwaiter
11 Distribution
12 Pantry
13 Dumbwaiter
14 Employees' dining room
15 Lounge
16 Freight elevator
17 Food storage
18 Cold storage

19 Kitchen
20 Dietary kitchen
21 Restaurant
22 Reception
23 Doctors' room
24 Waiting room
25 Lung X-ray ('Abreugrafia', a Brazilian process of mass miniature radiography)

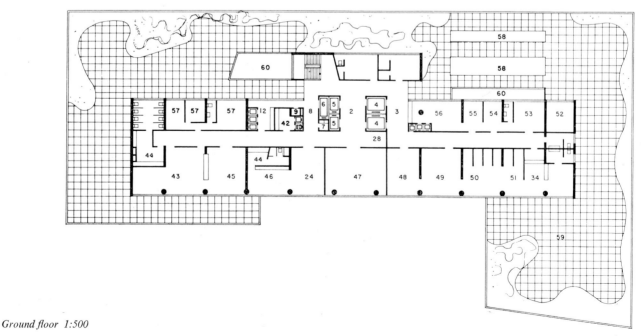

Ground floor 1:500

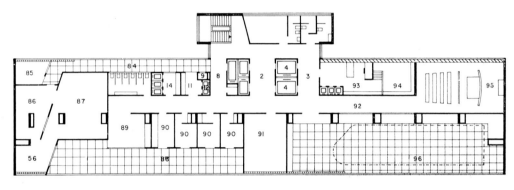

Second to ninth floor 1:500

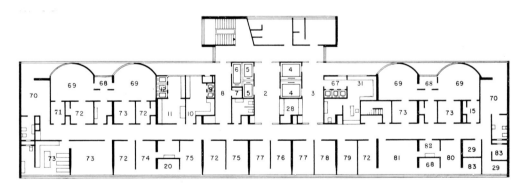

Eleventh floor 1:500

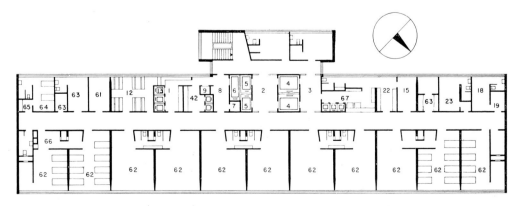

Twelfth floor 1:500

OSCAR NIEMEYER

Church of St. Francis / 1943 / Pampulha, Minas Gerais

Situated at the edge of the lake on the banks of which Niemeyer also planned a sports and recreation club (pages 166 to 171), this little church with its novel structural shapes, adapted to the technical possibilities of reinforced concrete, illustrates the urge for constant plastic research that distinguishes this artist and enables him to depart successfully from the more Cartesian conventions of modern architecture.

The nave is parabolic in section and decreases in rise from the front to the altar. On the inside it is faced with wood and on the outside with glazed mosaic tile in a composition by Paulo Werneck. The altar is roofed by another parabola, meeting three other parabolas, one on one side and two on the other, which contain the sacristy and other annexes. The altar is lighted by a clerestory above the parabola of the nave. The front, protected by a *brise-soleil* at the top, is connected by the sloping marquee to the bell-tower, dramatic outline of which contrasts with the curves that domina the design. The tile mural on the rear façade, depicting the life Saint Francis of Assisi, brother of all creatures, is by Portina who also painted the great altar fresco in which Christ is repr sented as the friend of the sick, the poor and the sinners, and stations of the Cross, hung along either side of the nave.

The construction of this church set off a storm of discussion, a for this reason it was never consecrated by the ecclesiastical a thorities. This opposition, which obliged the SPHAN to ta charge of the building (on the grounds that it really was a natio monument) seems even more extraordinary in our days, consid ing that a great International Eucharistic Congress was held in F de Janeiro before the modern altar shown on page 164.

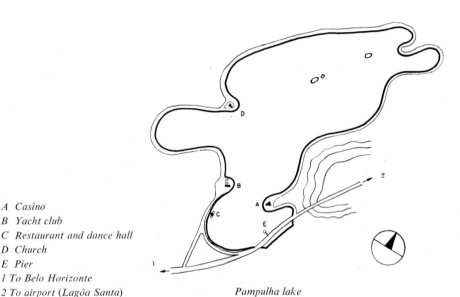

A Casino
B Yacht club
C Restaurant and dance hall
D Church
E Pier
1 To Belo Horizonte
2 To airport (*Lagôa Santa*)

Pampulha lake

Plan of church 1:500

Narthex
Nave
Altar
Priest
Sacristy
Bell tower

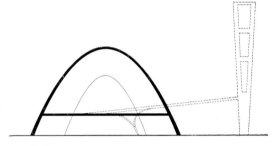

Section 1:400

161

FRANCISCO BOLONHA

St. Mary's Chapel in Ambassador Hildebrando Accioly's country house / 1954 / Fazenda Inglêsa, Petrópolis, Rio de Janeiro

In contrast to the church erected by Niemeyer, this chapel, forming part of a country house (page 40), relies on simpler, more primitive means to obtain, nevertheless, a high standard of refinement, as much in the general layout as in the design of each detail.

Connected to the main building by a large covered gallery, t[...] chapel stands out discreetly with its log front wall, even mo[...] rustic in design than the rest of the house. The mural is by Eme[...] Marcier and the interior decoration by D. Gerardo Martins, o. s. [...]

Section 1 1:400

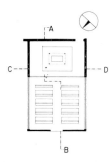

Plan 1:400

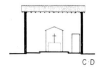

Section 2 1:400

ALCIDES ROCHA MIRANDA, ELVIN MCKAY DUBUGRAS *and* FERNANDO CABRAL PINTO

Altar Pavilion for the XXXVI International Eucharistic Congress / 1955 / Rio de Janeiro (Original design by Lúcio Costa)

This altar was the focal point of an important religious ceremony that gathered together close on a million pilgrims from all over the world. It was a temporary structure assembled at short notice on an earth fill advancing into Guanabara Bay in accordance with the plan for remodeling the waterfront in this part of the city, shown on page 230.

The construction, besides being extremely light, had to be almost entirely pre-fabricated in order to meet the requirements of the site and the close time schedule.

The broad horizontal lines of the design, carried out with the utmost simplicity from an original sketch by Lúcio Costa, furnish a background for the great wooden cross in front and to the left; the contrast with the huge sail billowing on the right and in back of the building is especially striking. Evoking the caravels of the Portuguese mariners on their voyages of discovery, this canvas filling proudly to the sea breeze and floodlighted at night when the most important ceremonies were being held, stood out against the dim waters of the bay, where the vessels of the Fleet lay at anchor, garlanded in electric lamps; the whole composition thus acquired a symbolism and a monumental dignity that rendered unnecessa any further emphasis on the altar pavilion, erected on an artific mound so as to be in full sight of the multitude. At one time the were almost half a million communicants, 230 000 women a 250 000 men assembled on the esplanade, which covered an a of 330 000 square meters (3 552 200 square feet), of which 230 0 square meters (2 475 800 square feet) were surfaced with aspha The altar itself stood in the center, surmounted by the long th roofline and set off by a baldachin partly hung from the ceilin with a row of seats on either side for the high dignitaries of Chur and State. In the central part behind it, the pavilion had tv stories: the chapel, the sacristy and a room for the cardinals we on a level with the top of the mound, where the radio booths we also installed; on the floor below, built into the earthwork, we private lobbies, sound control rooms, and a first aid station.

The pavilion was executed in timber on a steel framework, roof with corrugated fiber cement. The wood facings were mer waxed and polished, with the exception of the roof, the baldach and the screens, which were painted.

Steps
Altar stand
Altar
Credence
Cardinal Legate
Apostolic Nuncio
Patriarch of the Orient
Cardinals
Bishops
Cross (14 m. or 36' 6" high)
Booth and platform
Chapel with altar
Cardinals' room
Sacristy
Service stairway
Radio booths
Photographers
Dignitaries

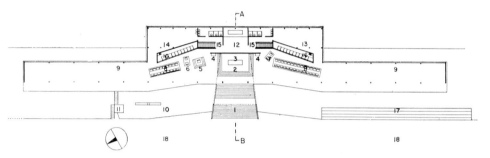

Plan 1:1000

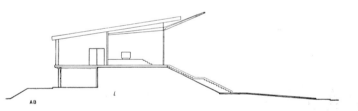

Section 1:500

OSCAR NIEMEYER

'Casa do Baile' dance hall / 1942 / Pampulha, Minas Gerais

The recreation and tourist center of Pampulha lies within easy reach of Belo Horizonte, capital of the state of Minas Gerais. The picturesque lake on which it is situated was made especially for the project by damming a broad, winding valley so as to form a sheet of water several miles long. It is interesting to note that the scheme was promoted by Juscelino Kubitschek de Oliveira when he was Mayor of the City, prior to taking office as Governor of Minas Gerais, for Brazil's new President has always been a great admirer of modern architecture. In addition to the three buildings now completed, the finished project will include a hotel, a golf club and other improvements. The 'Casa do Baile' is a small restaurant and popular dance hall on an island close to the dam and reached by a footbridge.

The hall is circular, but the crescent shape of the service areas built into it converts the floor plan into an ovoid. The roof a concrete slab, which is prolonged in flowing lines accompaing the shape of the island. At the extreme end of this windi marquee there is a lily pond with an open-air stage on the ot side of it, in line with the hall.

The contrast between the block, partly glazed and partly fac with a panel of *azulejos*, and the capricious outline of the m quee with its free structure clearly visible (typical of the architec uninhibited attitude towards form) expresses the convivial p pose of the program with an incomparably light touch. Construc in the period when the stimulating impact of modern architect was making itself most strongly felt, this building marked a spec trend that had a decisive influence on the thinking of youn architects.

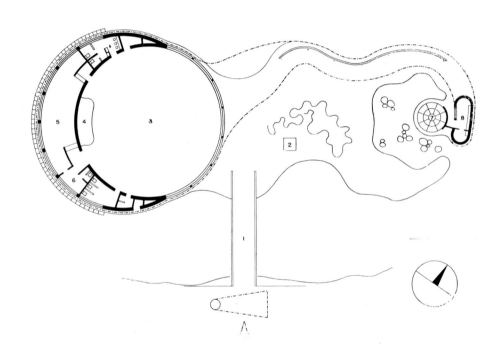

1 Gangway
2 Sculpture
3 Restaurant
4 Bandstand
5 Kitchen-Pantry
6 Employees' dining
7 Stage
8 Dressing room

Plan 1:500

OSCAR NIEMEYER

Casino / 1942 / Pampulha, Minas Gerais

This Casino, situated on a promontory jutting out from the lake-side, can be seen across the waters both from the 'Casa do Baile' and from the third unit in the project, the Yacht Club. The program includes the usual lounges, gaming-rooms, bar and restaurant, with a dance floor and stage, arranged in three clearly connected masses, expressing in simple forms, accurately outlined, the function of each part; any possible severity of the whole is transformed and tempered by the interplay of the communicating masses and by the transparency of the elevations and interiors, as well as by the *pilotis* and *brise-soleil* of the rounded block and the

playful outline of the canopy over the entrance, combined with sculpture by Zamoiski.

The outer columns are faced with travertine and the walls with ashlar. Inside, the columns clad in chromium-plated brass, the ramp parapets in Argentine onyx, the profusion of mirrors and all the decorative effects, even the under-surface lighting of the dance floor, help to create a suitable atmosphere in the building without resorting to the cheap effects so often used by many decorators in similar cases.

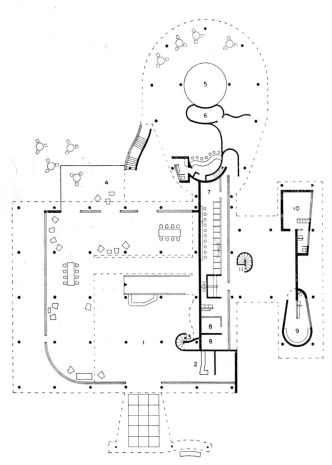

Ground floor 1:500

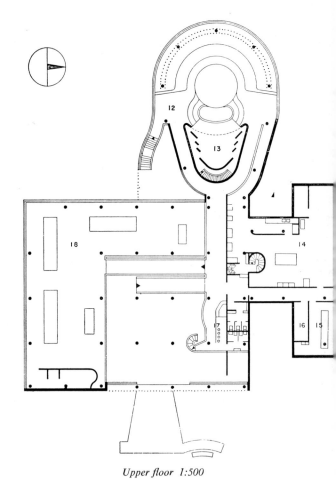

Upper floor 1:500

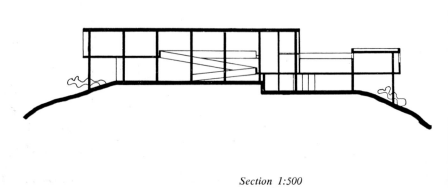

Section 1:500

Lobby
Check-room
Entrance to women's W.C.
Terrace
Dance floor
Storage
Dressing rooms
Private dressing room
Employees' lockers
Manager
Service stairway
Restaurant
Stage
Kitchen-Pantry
Employees' dining room
Storage
Bar
Gaming room

OSCAR NIEMEYER

Yacht Club / 1942 / Pampulha, Minas Gerais

The search for new forms, legitimately expressive of a contemporary program and suitable to modern techniques, is apparent in the other buildings of Pampulha, but in this example it reaches the highest level of integration of all the design elements. The cross-section of the inverted double-slope roof corresponds precisely to the two different volumes required inside on the upper story, which comprises a restaurant on one side and a large lounge on the other. The acoustic shell where the band plays is carried up to the ceiling of the restaurant, accompanying the slope of the roof. The two glazed façades that open onto the terrace over the boat-

house and onto the balcony leading to the access ramp, contra
with the blind wall at one end and the western façade protected
adjustable *brise-soleil*, designed in two bands, one above the oth
and on various planes, which gives a good idea of the versatili
of this architectural element.

The ground floor, part *pilotis* area and part enclosed boathouse,
faced with tiling in a traditional pattern and adequately suppo
the graceful, attractive silhouette of the main block.

The mural in the lounge is the work of Burle Marx.

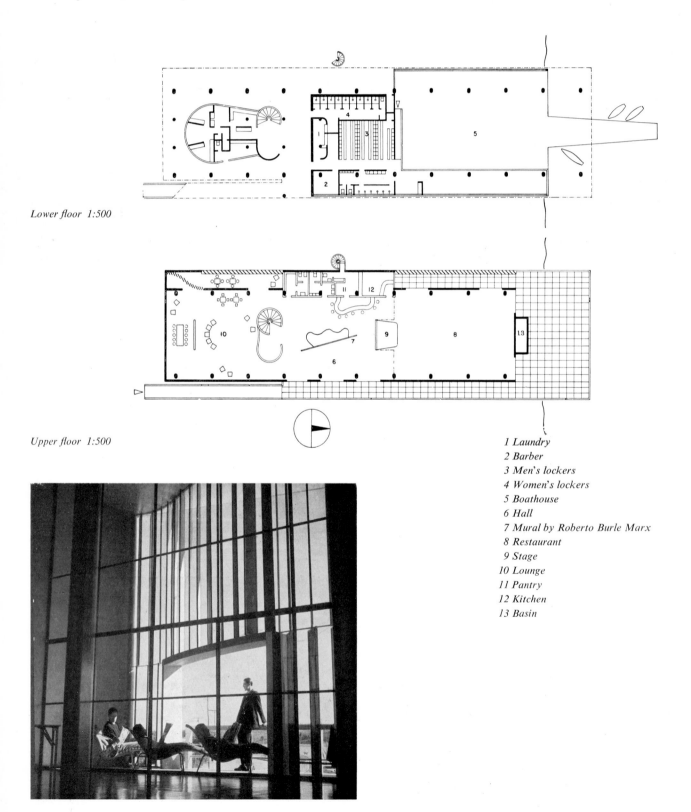

Lower floor 1:500

Upper floor 1:500

1 Laundry
2 Barber
3 Men's lockers
4 Women's lockers
5 Boathouse
6 Hall
7 Mural by Roberto Burle Marx
8 Restaurant
9 Stage
10 Lounge
11 Pantry
12 Kitchen
13 Basin

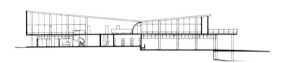

Section 1:1000

AFFONSO EDUARDO REIDY

Community theater in the Marechal Hermes district / 1950 / Rio de Janeiro

In this attractive community theater, erected by the City of Rio de Janeiro in an industrial suburb for staging popular productions by professionals and amateurs, the inverted double slope roof again helps to give an appropriately cheerful appearance to the design, while integrating in form the external aspect with the internal layout.

The interpenetration of the two roof slopes corresponds to the auditorium section and serves a dual purpose: to the rear of the building this arrangement allows sufficient height for the stage with its scenery and cyclorama, while to the front it enables the lobby to be lighted by a clerestory, the public toilets on the mezzanine being also lighted by windows invisible from the outside.

The design includes a lobby, an auditorium seating 300, a stor room, an office, and a stage with room for stacking scenery. T toilets on the mezzanine are reached by circular staircases show on the plan. The dressing rooms are in a small block, connecte to the back of the main building by the stage door lobby, ar balance, in the design, the concrete marquee, supported on ste tubing, which projects outward and upward from the main e trance.

The panel on the side wall is by Paulo Werneck, and the garde was landscaped by Burle Marx, who also designed the stage curta woven by Lili Correia de Araújo.

1 Ticket office
2 Billboard
3 Lobby
4 Check-room
5 Cyclorama

6 Management
7 Wardrobe
8 Performers' entrance
9 Service entrance
10 Dressing rooms

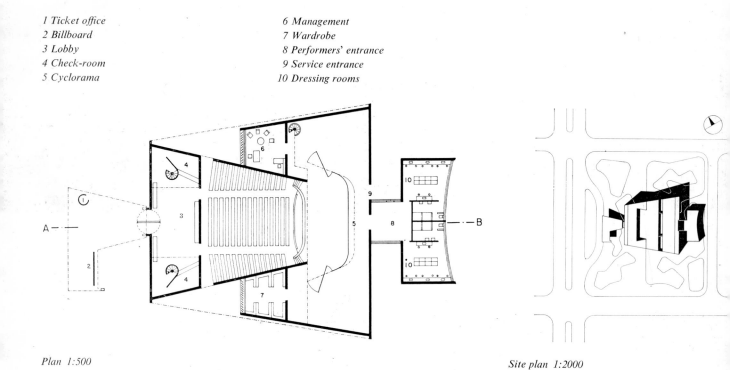

Plan 1:500

Site plan 1:2000

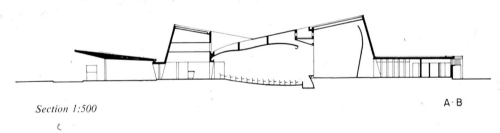

Section 1:500   A·B

PEDRO PAULÔ BASTOS, RAFAEL GALVÃO, ANTÔNIO DIAS CARNEIRO, ORLANDO AZEVEDO *architec*

Antônio Alves de Noronha, Paulo Fragoso, Sergio Marques de Souza *and* **Colonel Alberto Rodrigues da Costa** *structural designers*

Maracanã Municipal Stadium / 1950 / Rio de Janeiro

This stadium, remarkable for its size and the clear, simple solution given to the functional problems, is nearing completion and will form part of a sports center which is to include: a gymnasium (in construction), a swimming pool, stadia for athletics and choral singing, tennis and basketball courts, a shooting gallery and a children's playground. It has a normal seating capacity of 150 000 persons, distributed as follows: standing-room for 30 000 on the first tier of the stand; 30 000 numbered seats on the second tier; rows of benches seating 86 500 on the third tier; 2 500 special seats; 150 seats for distinguished visitors; and 850 seats in the press, radio and TV galleries.

Public access to the stand is by ramps and galleries leading separately to each tier and ingeniously arranged, starting from floor level, so as to enable all the spectators to be evacuated to the galleries in 15 minutes and from the galleries to the ground in 20 minutes. The inner ramps to the numbered seats have a width of 8 meters (about 26′ 3″) and the outer ramps 14 meters (45′ 11″). The special seats, distinguished visitors' and press galleries have elevator service. The various horizontal corridors are not open to the public, but are merely provided with staircases for service and police requirements. Perfect visibility from all seats and standing room was secured by means of a profile curve giving different heights for all the steps; this curve was worked out by Engineer Haroldo Lisbôa da Cunha.

A great number of the seats are under cover; the 14,6 meter (47′ 10″) overhang of the third tier provides protection for th second, while the third tier itself has a roof canopy with an ove hang of 30 meters (98′ 5″).

The structure is on an imposing scale and accompanies the shap of the stadium—an ellipse with a major axis of 300,5 meters (98 feet) and a minor axis of 262,84 meters (862 feet); the outer risin members lean outwards, giving a 'basket' silhouette to the buildin, so as to compensate the enormous overhang of the tiers. Th longest ramp has a gradient of 1 in 10 and is 236 meters (775 feet the topmost tread being only 23,6 meters (about 77 feet) abov ground level.

The tier for standing spectators is separated from the arena by pit 3,5 meters (about 11′ 6″) deep. In the basement there ar lodgings and annexes for two teams of 75 athletes and for the refe ees, with access completely independent from that available to th public; there are also first aid stations for athletes and public, an parking space is provided for ambulances. The arena is reache by tunnels.

The intermediate floors house the social and administrative serv ices, and lodgings for athletes in training, with departments o medico-biometrics, mechanotherapy, electrotherapy, traumatc logy, X-rays, etc. Along the horizontal corridors corresponding t each tier, there are wash-rooms, bars, restaurants and workroom, bookstalls, souvenir and sporting goods stores, public telephone and post and telegraph offices.

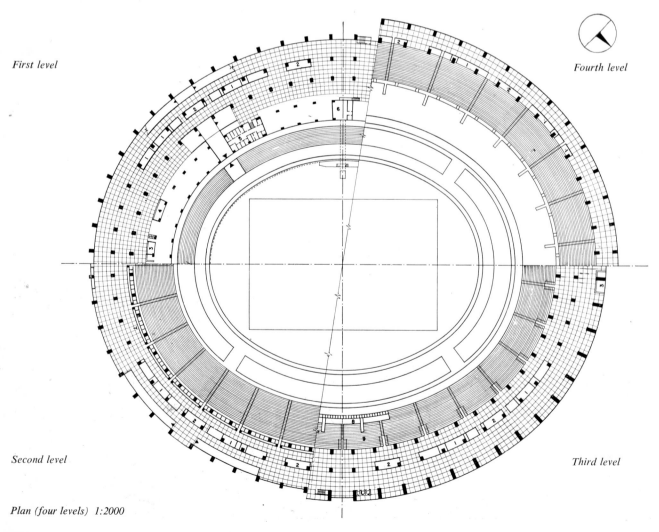

First level

Fourth level

Second level

Third level

Plan (four levels) 1:2000

Toilets
Bar
Press (Radio, Post Office and Telegraph)
Sports goods
Medical service
Photographers
Boxes
Press booth
Official guests

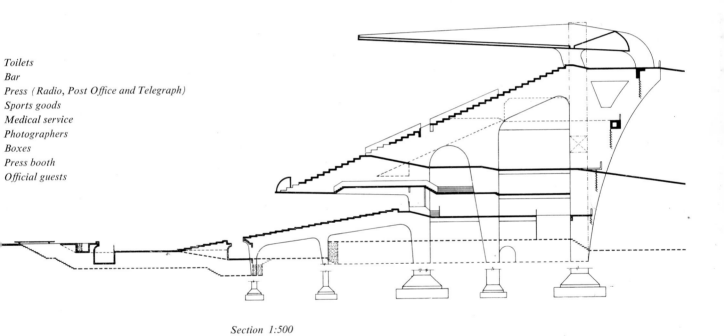

Section 1:500

ICARO DE CASTRO MELLO

Indoor swimming pool / 1952 / São Paulo

This covered swimming pool built by the São Paulo State Sports Department has a seating capacity of 4500 spectators. The water in the pool is heated to 26° C. (79° F.) to enable athletes to train in the cold climate of São Paulo.

The architect, who is well known for this type of construction, has convincingly expressed, in terms of volume, both the purpose of the building and the arrangement, in plan, of the stands on either side of the 25 × 18 meter (82 × 59 foot) pool.

The reinforced concrete structure, made up of parabolic arche tied by pre-assembled hollow brick elements, is roofed in alum num sheets over a wooden structure supported by the arches The space below the stands is occupied by the dressing rooms an showers for men and women swimmers, public toilets and a ba The filters and pumps of the processing plant are located at on end of the pool, with the boilers for heating the water in a smal annex near the building.

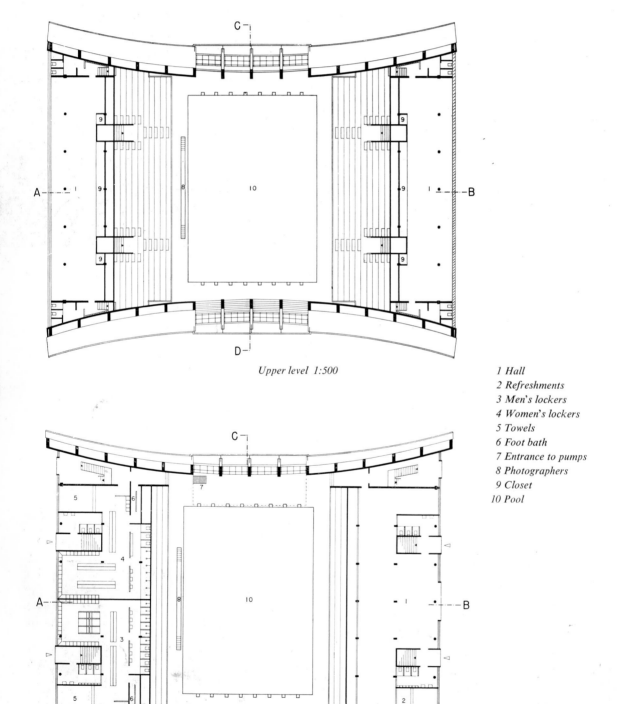

Upper level 1:500

Lower level 1:500

1 Hall
2 Refreshments
3 Men's lockers
4 Women's lockers
5 Towels
6 Foot bath
7 Entrance to pumps
8 Photographers
9 Closet
10 Pool

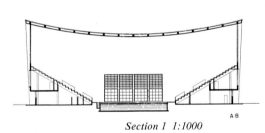

Section 1 1:1000

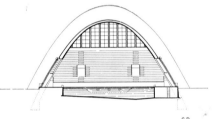

Section 2 1:1000

OLAVO REDIG DE CAMPOS

Swimming pavilion at the country house of Homero Souza e Silva / 1955 / Petrópolis, Rio de Janeiro

The need for wind and rain protection was used here as a pretext for a demonstration of the possibilities of reinforced concrete, which gives this pavilion a gay, playful character.

The dressing rooms are on a lower level, partially concealed by the lay of the land, and connected with the upper level by a staircase that follows the curving lines of the shelter. A small kitchen ne[ar] the dressing rooms is connected with the bar by a dumbwaiter. On the opposite side of the pool, the designer has made use of a[n] old stone wall as a background for a mural in glass mosaic [by] Laszlo Meitner and the cheerful colors are reflected in the water.

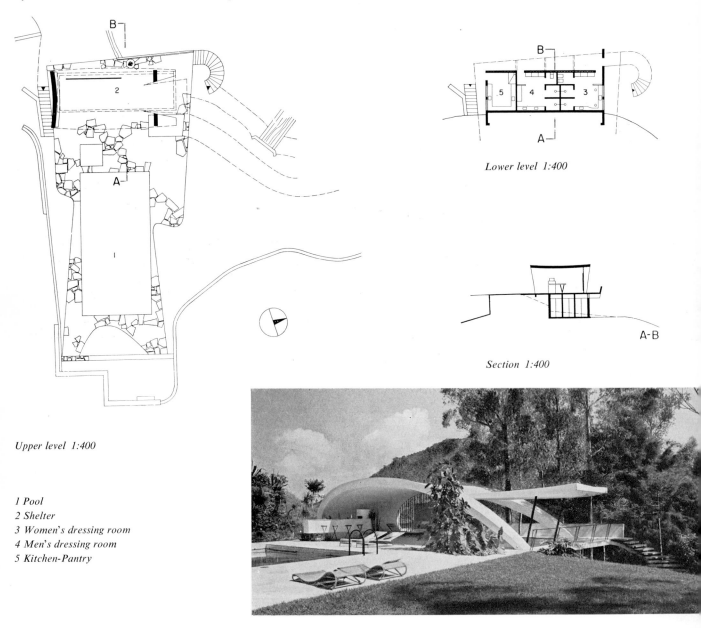

Lower level 1:400

Section 1:400

Upper level 1:400

1 Pool
2 Shelter
3 Women's dressing room
4 Men's dressing room
5 Kitchen-Pantry

imming pavilion at the country house of Alfredo Baumann / 1955 / Vale da Bôa Esperança, near Petrópolis, Rio de Janeiro

contrast to the preceding example, a strict discipline here re-
ces the elements of design to the essential minimum.
simple concrete slab, supported on a wall of boulders and on
n posts, partially roofs a deck of granite flagstones laid on
ulders, adjoining an L-shaped swimming pool. The closed-in
area has a board floor and is protected on three sides by glazed
walls.

The design of the pavilion was worked out in close connection
with the plans for the garden, which is being landscaped by Burle
Marx.

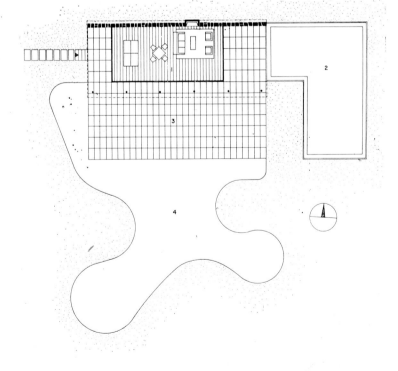

1 Lounge
2 Pool
3 Terrace
4 Pond

Plan 1:400

LÚCIO COSTA *and* OSCAR NIEMEYER, *with* PAUL LESTER WIENER

Brazilian Pavilion at the New York World's Fair / 1939 / New York

Standing out among the other buildings of the Fair, this pavilion, unfortunately a temporary construction like that of Mies van der Rohe in the Barcelona Exhibition of 1929, focussed world-wide attention on the work of modern Brazilian architects, who, at that time, had few completed works to display.

The light, cheerful lines, uniting outside and inside in interpenetrating volumes and creating an astonishing richness of perspective at every level, appeared unexpectedly in the midst of the indiscriminate confusion of styles produced by the other buildings in the Fair and proved to be one of the rare instances of true architectural merit.

The ground floor, containing a restaurant and dance floor, w assigned to the flora and fauna of Brazil and included, in t garden, an aviary, an orchidarium, an aquarium and a lily po with a snake pit. The upper floor, reached by two stairways and outer ramp, had a capacious terrace, partially roofed over, w a small auditorium. The terrace led onto the main exhibition ha with a mezzanine as shown on the plan.

The fixed egg-crate panel on the southern façade is one of the e ments that call to mind the fruitful teaching of Le Corbus during the planning of the Ministry of Education building.

1 Restaurant
2 Dance floor
3 Kitchen-Pantry
4 Café
5 Exhibitions
6 Information
7 Aviary
8 Storage
9 Fish pool
10 Orchids
11 Snakes
12 Office
13 Auditorium

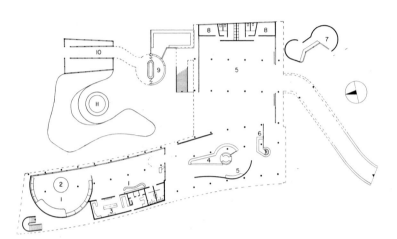

Lower floor 1:1000

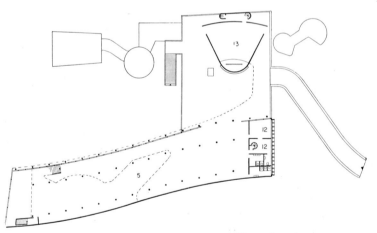

Upper floor 1:1000

180

LINA BO BARDI

São Paulo Museum of Art / 1947 / São Paulo

The same office building in the center of town houses both this museum, created in October 1947 by Assis Chateaubriand, the owner of a chain of newspapers, radio and TV stations, and managed by P. M. Bardi, and, temporarily, the São Paulo Museum of Modern Art, created by Mr. and Mrs. Francisco Matarazzo Sobrinho, which has earned world-wide renown through the Biennials (three have now been held: 1951, 1953 and 1955), as well as by the International Exhibitions of Architecture.

The São Paulo Museum of Art, which possesses a permanent collection covering all periods of the history of art, is also an important center of instruction in all branches of esthetic creation. The wide range of subjects taught there includes musicology, dancing, industrial design, advertising and handicrafts. There are also courses for children.

The two floors illustrated contain: below, a small auditorium and a larger one (seating 300), galleries for temporary and educational exhibits, administrative offices, a library and a photographic laboratory; above, the main art galleries. The various courses referred to are given on other floors of the same building.

The main exhibition floor is uniformly lighted from the ceiling an egg-crate of white enameled metal strips subdivided into s[...] tions swinging right back so as to allow for easy cleaning a[...] repair of the fluorescent lighting fixtures. The mounting of [...] display screens on steel tubing with guy and turnbuckle adjustm[...] ensures minimum encumbrance of the gallery and maximum fle[...] bility in use. As the windows on either side do not supply enou[...] light, they are only used for cross ventilation and masked [...] venetian blinds which create a uniform background. On the lov[...] floor, the smaller of the auditoriums is equipped with an acous[...] canopy hung from the ceiling and drapes of woven materia[...] The ceiling of the larger auditorium is covered with inclir[...] wooden slates, in venetian blind arrangement and painted whi[...] this allows the air to circulate freely and ensures good acousti[...] the draperies are blue cotton.

The continuity and transparency of the bays, and the simplic[...] and good taste observed in every detail, without impairing fu[...] tional efficiency, produce a feeling of spaciousness that is partic[...] larly pleasing.

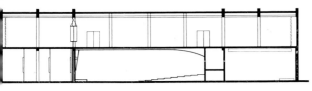

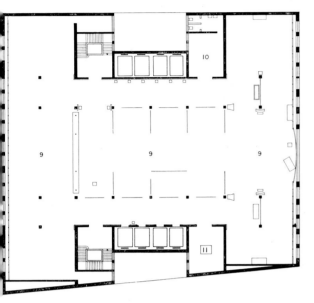

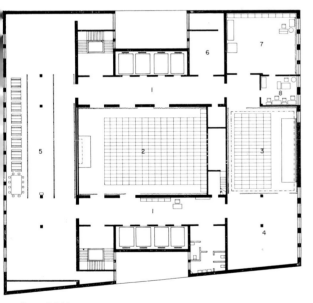

Gallery
Auditorium
Smaller auditorium
Small exhibitions
Large exhibitions
Photographic laboratory
Curator and library
Secretary
Permanent collection
Tapestry collection
Storage

OSCAR NIEMEYER, ZENON LOTUFO, HELIO UCHÔA *and* EDUARDO KNEESE DE MELLO

Associate architects GAUSS ESTELITA *and* CARLOS LEMOS

Palaces of Nations and States (Ibirapuéra Park) / 1951 / São Paulo

The ensemble of Ibarapuéra Park, designed for the festival in commemoration of the Fourth Centennial of the Foundation of the City of São Paulo, has not been entirely completed. The Auditorium (page 189) is missing, and with it the connection of the big marquee to the Palace of Arts and to the Auditorium, as well as the gardens planned by Burle Marx.

Had it been entirely finished, it would have provided a rare example of integral and harmonious planning applied to a set of permanent buildings for exhibitions and fairs of every kind, spread over a wide area suitably landscaped.

The Palace of Nations and the Palace of States (3 and 4 on the plan on page 192) are located at right angles to one another and are chiefly intended for plastic art exhibitions. The famous Biennials were held there in 1953 and 1955; not only the exhibitions but also this entire project was promoted by Mr. and Mrs. Francisco Matarazzo Sobrinho.

Each of the two buildings, identical in plan, comprises an enormous hall (about 140 × 42 meters or 460 × 138 feet) on the upper story,

with 5 meters (16′ 5″) headroom, and another on the grou⟨nd⟩ floor with 4 meters (13′ 1½″) headroom and a sunken cent⟨er⟩ part 2 meters (6′ 6¾″) lower.

The open *pilotis* area on the ground floor is generally used a⟨s⟩ bar and café. The two blocks, each 150 meters (492 feet) in leng⟨th⟩ are incorporated in the general composition by two extensions⟨of⟩ the large marquee (page 192). The roof slab is protected ⟨by⟩ aluminum sheets.

Public access is by ramps. The 10 meter (32′ 10″) distance ⟨be⟩tween columns in either direction of the free structure in re⟨in⟩forced concrete enables exhibitions to be organized with ⟨the⟩ greatest flexibility by the use of movable panels. The columns alo⟨ng⟩ the glazed façades of the upper story are supported by reinfor⟨ced⟩ concrete brackets, with the feet of the struts connected at grou⟨nd⟩ level to the second row of columns. Thus the lightness of the upp⟨er⟩ block, silhouetted as a plain concrete frame surrounding the i⟨m⟩mense glazed panel, is enhanced by the sloping lines of the low⟨er⟩ structure.

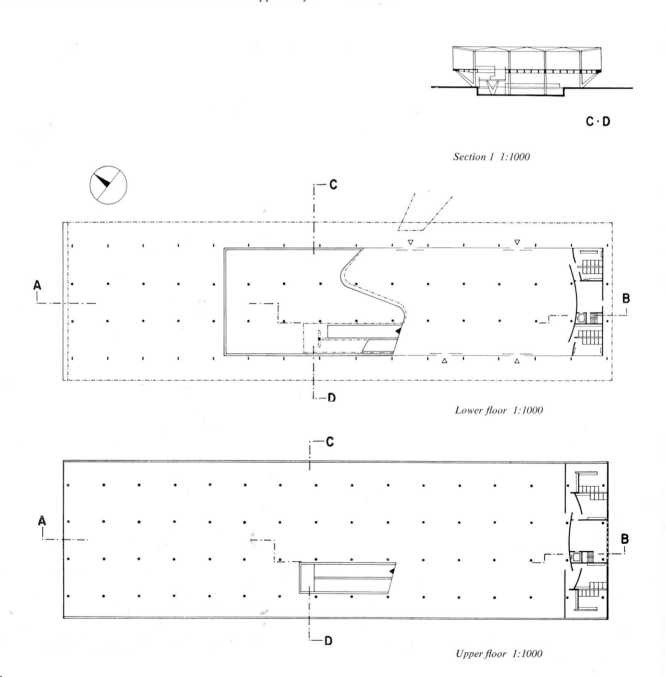

C·D

Section 1 1:1000

Lower floor 1:1000

Upper floor 1:1000

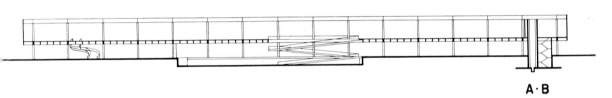

Section 2 1:1000

A·B

OSCAR NIEMEYER, ZENON LOTUFO, HELIO UCHÔA *and* **EDUARDO KNEESE DE MELLO**

Associate architects **GAUSS ESTELITA** *and* **CARLOS LEMOS**

Palace of Industry (Ibirapuéra Park) / 1953 / São Paulo

Located at the opposite end of the big marquee, the Palace of Industry, intended for exhibits of machinery and manufactured products, covers an area of 250 × 50 meters (about 820 × 164 feet).

The slope of the land is slight, but appreciable because of the length of the block, so that at one end the ground floor has a ceiling height of 8,6 meters (28′ 2″). This end is open, with *pilotis*, and has a mezzanine running back to form the ground floor at the other end of the building, with a ceiling height of 4 meters (13′ 1½″). The two stories above this are each 5 meters (16′ 5″) high.

The same basic distance between columns, 10 meters (32′ 10″)

either way, is used in this block and in the Palaces of Nations an States.

Communication between floors is assured by escalators and tw ramps, an inner and an outer one. The northeastern façade is part ally protected by adjustable vertical *brise-soleil* made of aluminur The capricious outline of the slabs at the end of the mezzanine, ar around the inner ramp that accedes to the upper stories, as well the structure of the ramp itself, helps to give the interior an imagi ative and spectacular look contrasting with the impressive sobrie of the outside treatment, the simplicity of which accentuates th unusually large scale of the building.

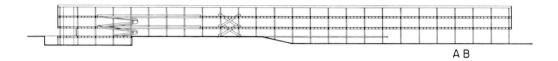

Section 1 1:2000

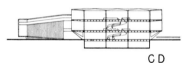

Section 2 1:2000

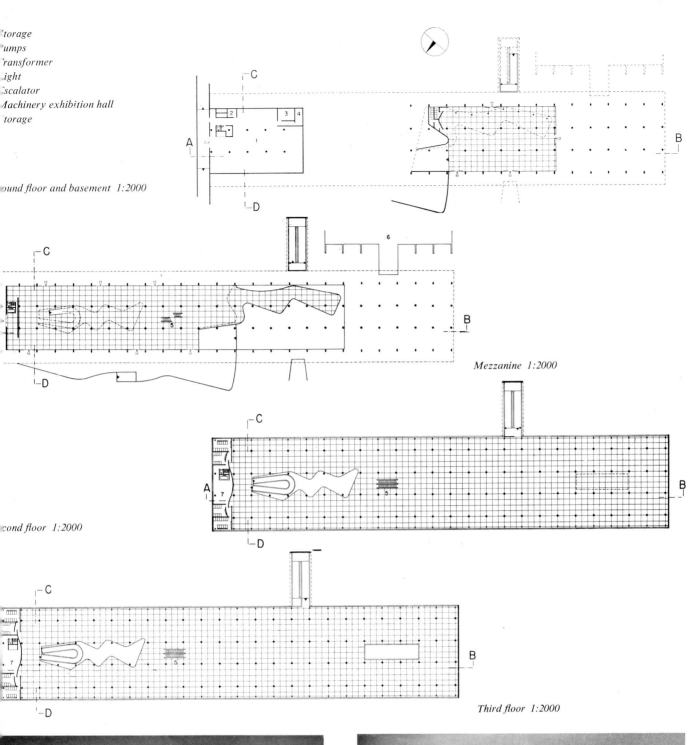

ound floor and basement 1:2000

6

Mezzanine 1:2000

cond floor 1:2000

Third floor 1:2000

OSCAR NIEMEYER, ZENON LOTUFO, HELIO UCHÔA *and* **EDUARDO KNEESE DE MELLO**
Associate architects **GAUSS ESTELITA** *and* **CARLOS LEMOS**

Palace of the Arts (Ibirapuéra Park) / 1954 / São Paulo

If there is a touch of the spectacular in the treatment of the Palace of Industry, inside this unit, specially designed for sculpture exhibitions, the effect is truly Wellsian, a kind of optimistic projection into a future less subject to the stringent demands of gravity or at least to their conventional interpretation.

Below the dome, which emerges from the site and is illuminated by 30 skylights located along the periphery almost at ground level, two concrete platforms, one rectangular and the other hexagonal, both with concave edges, seem to be suspended from their corners.

The open spaces between the sides of these platforms and the inner surface of the dome combine with the openings in the ground floor giving onto the floor below and with the horseshoe ramp connecting all four levels (in addition to the escalators) to provide a changing play of perspectives that contrasts strikingly with the monolithic aspect of the construction when viewed from without. The Auditorium, completing the design of this part of the ensemble and justifying the shape of the big marquee at this point, remains to be built.

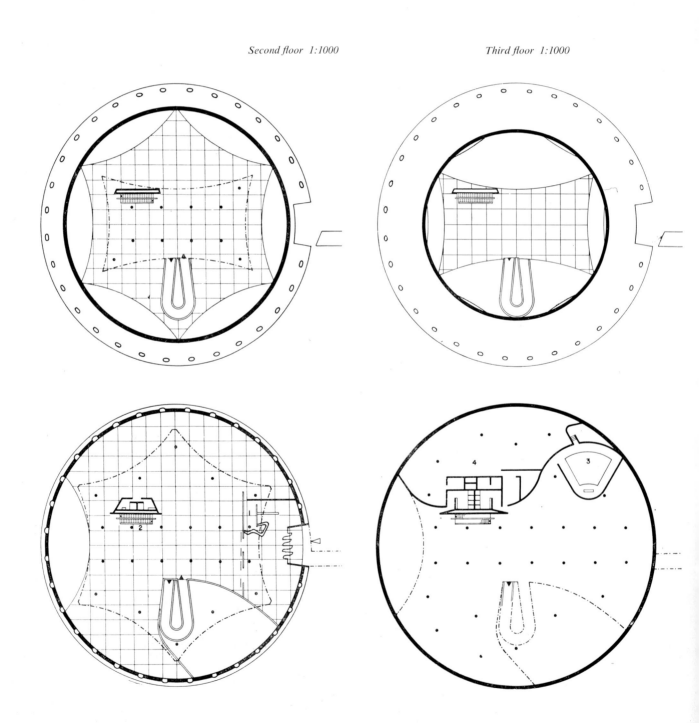

Second floor 1:1000

Third floor 1:1000

Ground floor 1:1000

Basement 1:1000

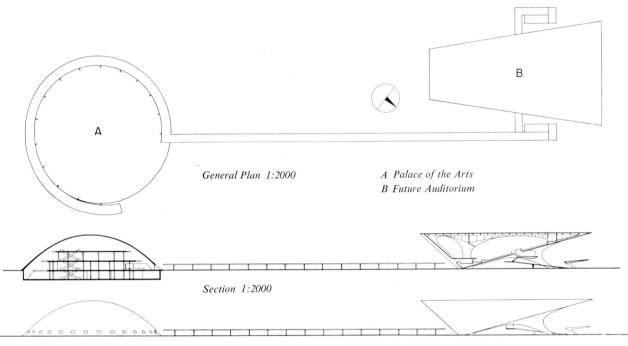

General Plan 1:2000   A Palace of the Arts
                                 B Future Auditorium

Section 1:2000

Elevation (Palace of the Arts and Auditorium) 1:2000

OSCAR NIEMEYER, ZENON LOTUFO, HELIO UCHÔA and **EDUARDO KNEESE DE MELLO**

Associate architects **GAUSS ESTELITA** *and* **CARLOS LEMOS**

Palace of Agriculture (Ibirapuéra Park) / 1955 / São Paulo

This building designed for the Department of Agriculture of the State of São Paulo is also situated in Ibirapuéra Park and forms an integral part of the project.

The ground floor, with the V-columns adopted by Niemeyer in much of his recent work, has 6,3 meters (20′ 8″) of headroom and a mezzanine (with a lecture hall) carried out from the front of the building to roof the restaurant annex. The building block comprises seven typical floors for the various departments, each 3,5 meters (11′ 6″) high, and a top floor with living quarters for transient officials. Public access to the various floors is pro-

vided inside the block, entirely independent of personnel traffi for which there is a tower annexed to the rear façade. The floo measure 130 × 18,5 meters (426′ 6″ × 60′ 8″) and are su ported by two rows of pillars, 12 meters (39′ 4″) apart with distance between pillars of 6 meters (19′ 8″), thus forming two i dependent circulation galleries along the façades, one for th public and the other for the personnel.

The northwestern façade will be protected from top to bottom b adjustable vertical *brise-soleil* in aluminum.

1 Employees' hall
2 Public hall
3 Private entrance hall for the Secretary
   of Agriculture
4 Pantry
5 Exhibitions
6 Bar
7 Kitchen-Pantry
8 Restaurant
9 Waiting room
10 Lecture room
11 Terrace (Restaurant roof)
12 Offices
13 Reception and information
14 Employees' circulation
15 Public circulation
16 Reception
17 Waiting room
18 Linen
19 Bedroom
20 Lounge
21 Bar

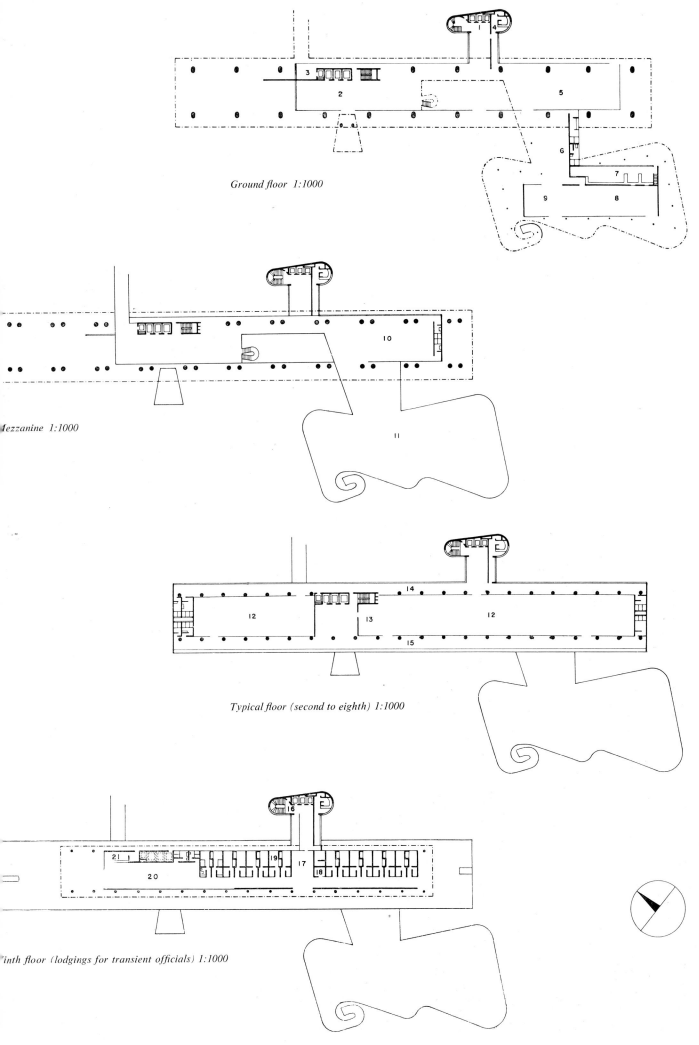

Ground floor 1:1000

Mezzanine 1:1000

Typical floor (second to eighth) 1:1000

Ninth floor (lodgings for transient officials) 1:1000

191

OSCAR NIEMEYER, ZENON LOTUFO, HELIO UCHÔA *and* EDUARDO KNEESE DE MELLO
Associate architects **GAUSS ESTELITA** *and* **CARLOS LEMOS**

Big Marquee (Ibirapuéra Park) / 1951-55 / São Paulo

This huge marquee of reinforced concrete, supported on slender columns, forms a covered promenade for visitors, linking all the buildings and stressing the unity of the whole, set neatly and precisely amid the capricious landscaping of the park. Freely designed in flowing lines, it presents, at any point, a dynamic perspectiv[e] contrasting with the quiet stability of the various blocks.

In the photograph of the model below, the Palace of Agricultu[re] can be seen in the lower left-hand corner.

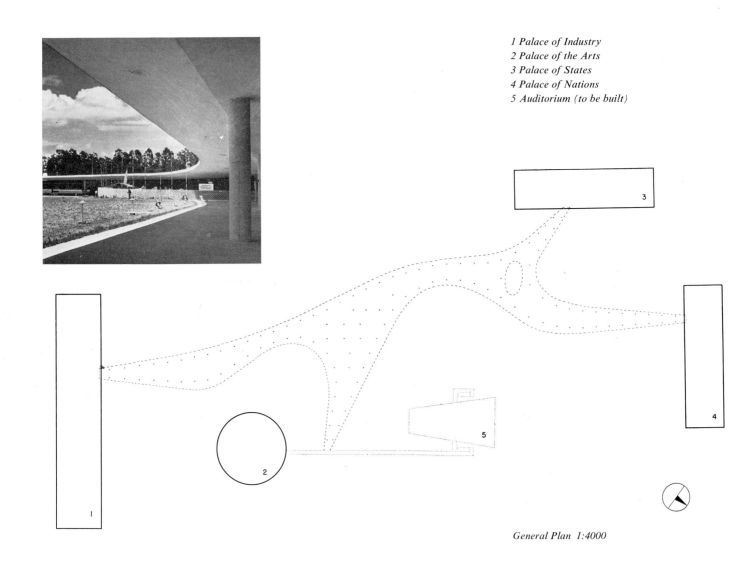

1 Palace of Industry
2 Palace of the Arts
3 Palace of States
4 Palace of Nations
5 Auditorium (to be built)

General Plan 1:4000

Administration, Business

Industry

M. M. ROBERTO

A B I Building (Associação Brasileira de Imprensa – Brazilian Press Association) – Herbert Moses Building / 1938 / Rio de Janeiro

This building was the first example of modern architecture in Brazil to be carried out on a large scale. The architects, chosen by competition in 1936, developed the project originally submitted with practically no modification. The only important change was the substitution of the *brise-soleil*, intended to be duralumin, by pre-cast reinforced concrete slabs plastered with white cement. The high-grade finish, designed for permanence, contrasts with the lower standard unfortunately imposed on so many other works by the speculative nature of such undertakings.

The system of protection against an excess of sunlight consists of bands of *brise-soleil* covering both façades and separated from the outer walls of the rooms (made up of glazed doors with top ventilation) by a corridor that not only allows for auxiliary circulation, but acts as a heat dispersion zone.

With the exception of the shop space on the ground floor and the four floors for rental (2nd to 5th), the building is occupied by the Brazilian Press Association (or 'A B I'), which thus disposes of one floor for offices, with a small lecture room, one floor for the libra, one for the lounge and recreation rooms, one for a large audi rium and art exhibition gallery, and, at the top, a restaurant a roof garden (designed by Burle Marx).

The covered driveway on the left side of the open portico on t ground floor leads to an inner courtyard for parking purpos common to all the buildings in the block and a consequence of C planning throughout the Castelo zone (a section of governm and office buildings created within the last thirty years on the s of the hill of the same name which was leveled to provide fill new land reclaimed from the bay).

The two façades are faced with Argentine travertine marble; *pilotis* and the portico walls with Brazilian granite. In the eleva well, on the ground floor, the outer wall is faced with alumin sheet; this is replaced by plywood on the other floors, wh this facing is repeated on the adjacent walls of rooms and corrido

1 Portico
2 Shop
3 Members' room
4 Parking
5 W.C.
6 Librarian
7 Pantry
8 Writing room
9 Reading room
10 Archives
11 Book stacks
12 Storage
13 Check-room
14 Bar
15 Auditorium
16 Exhibitions
17 Barbershop
18 Information
19 Reading room
20 Lounge
21 Terrace
22 Game room

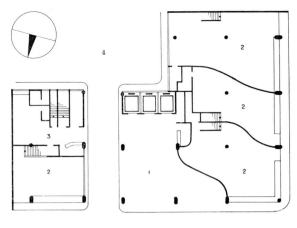

ground floor 1:500

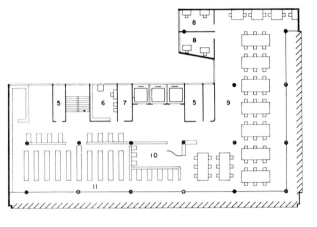

eighth floor 1:500

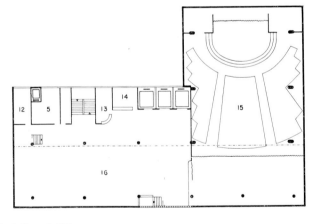

tenth floor 1:500

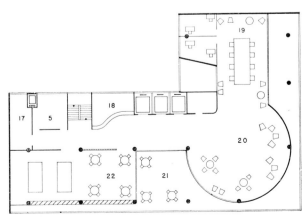

eleventh floor 1:500

LÚCIO COSTA, OSCAR NIEMEYER, CARLOS AZEVEDO LEÃO, JORGE MOREIRA, AFFONSO EDUARDO REIDY *and* **ERNANI VASCONCELOS, (LE CORBUSIER** *consultant*)

Ministry of Education and Health building / 1937-1943 / Rio de Janeiro

The building of the Ministry of Education is the most striking symbol of modern architecture in Brazil and the first application, on a monumental scale, of Le Corbusier's ideas. It clearly shows the strength with which a building can carve out the space around it, and at the same time provides a spectacular example of what an urban center might be, if it were not for the predominance of short-range speculative interests.

The strict plastic discipline applied to every component and the concision of the formal means employed, make every detail unequivocally subordinate to the design as a whole. All this thoroughly justifies the unparalleled importance that this work has acquired in the landscape of modern architecture in Brazil and the interest, emulation and discussion it has aroused abroad.

The fourteen-story block rises in the middle of the site on *pilotis* 10 meters (32′ 10″) high and rests at one end on a low transversal wing, containing an Auditorium on one side and a large Art Ex-, hibition Hall on the other; at the opposite end it covers a small three-story service annex with an entrance lobby from which the personnel elevators rise to the upper floors. The land area is far from overcrowded and so, from every angle, wide vistas with landscaped gardens meet the eye, enhanced rather than obstructed by the *pilotis*. Thus the capacity of this city lot, instead of being filled by the usual agglomeration of massive buildings lining the sidewalks, has an ample margin of free space to be used for the rational, practical purpose of bathing the edifice in light, air an sunshine and providing a suitable setting for the monumentalit of the design, a monumentality that is a true expression of th program, yet is so rarely attained by contemporary architects.

The plan of the typical floor, with three rows of columns, allow for the utmost flexibility in the interior layout on either side of central corridor running from the public elevators at one end t the personnel elevators at the other. The toilets and staircases ar also located at either end wall, so as not to encroach on the fre floor space.

One of the elevators in the group assigned to the public is reserve for the use of the Minister and Heads of Departments. The firs typical floor in the block has a higher ceiling than the others an contains the Ministerial suite, which opens onto the roof garde over the Exhibition Hall and here there is a reclining statue b Celso Antonio. A large wall fresco enriches the very large waitin lounge and a series of smaller frescoes are in the conference room All frescoes are by Portinari.

At a height of 17 stories above street level, the restaurants for th personnel and heads of departments are located in a roof garde above which rise the towers for the reservoirs and elevator hoist crowning the building with their curving walls faced in blue tile.

On the ground floor and on the second floor, the granite facing the broad glazed walls and the panels of *azulejos*, designed b

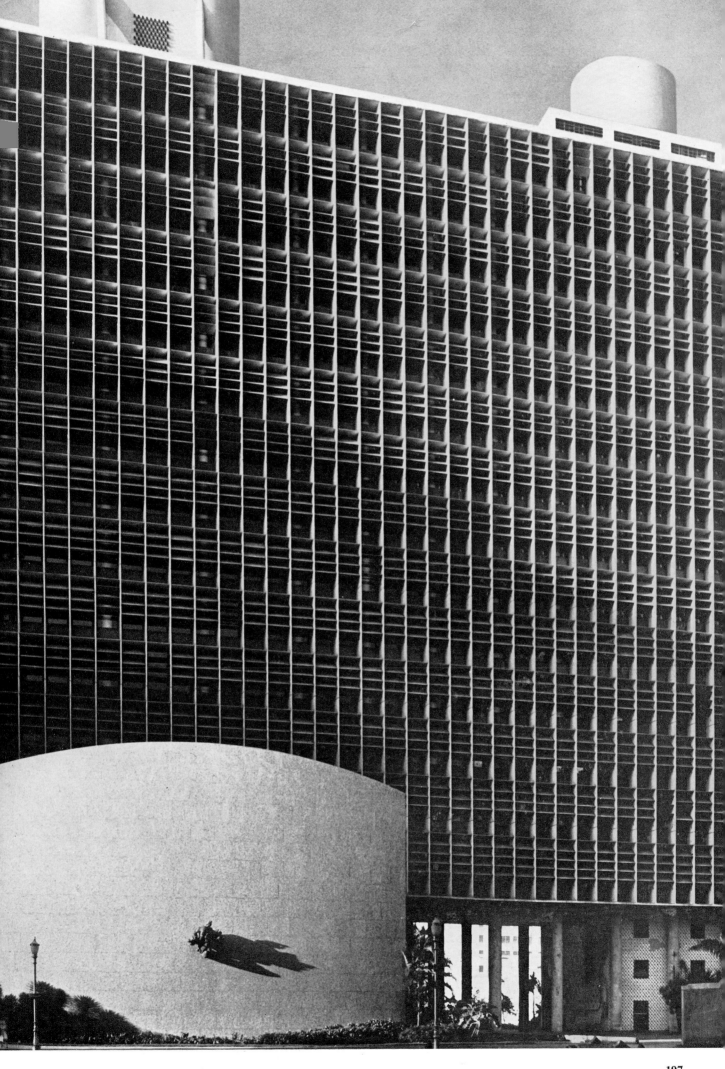

Portinari and executed by Paulo Rossi Osir, stress the plastic function of each unit with grace and dignity.

The building is finally characterized by two imposing blind walls, one at either end of the high block, faced with granite and contrasting with the great southeast wall, completely glazed, and that on the northwest, protected by movable horizontal *brise-soleil* in fiber cement sheet with metal framing, set in a pattern of thin horizontal and vertical concrete fins.

A sculptural group portraying 'Youth', by Bruno Giorgi, stands on the esplanade to the south, while on the other side a 'Prome-theus Unbound', by Jacques Lipchitz, is hung on the curved wall of the auditorium block. The latter work of art was unfortunately cast to one third the dimensions planned, with the result that its volume is twenty-seven times smaller than the sculptor expected; this certainly mars the effect and makes it look too small for the supporting wall.

Near the Ministry of Education stands the old church of Santa Luzia shown on the frontispiece. The *vue d'ensemble* of these two buildings, the old and the new, sums up the atmosphere in which architecture develops in Brazil.

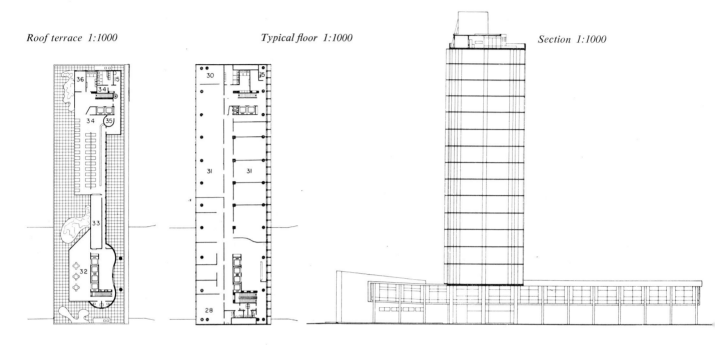

Roof terrace 1:1000 *Typical floor 1:1000* *Section 1:1000*

1 Reception
2 Incinerator
3 Employees' private entrance
4 Reception
5 Public hall
6 Minister's entrance
7 Power
8 Treasury
9 Air conditioning
10 Flagpole
11 Sculpture
12 Storage
13 Switchboard
14 General storage
15 Pantry
16 Exhibition workroom
17 Exhibitions
18 Lecture room
19 Auditorium
20 Projection booth
21 Waiting room
22 Minister's office
23 Assistant
24 Despatch room
25 Chief assistant
26 Offices
27 Reception and Information
28 Press and Radio
29 Staff
30 Director
31 Office area
32 Minister's dining room
33 Kitchen
34 Employees' dining room
35 Building superintendent
36 Lockers

198

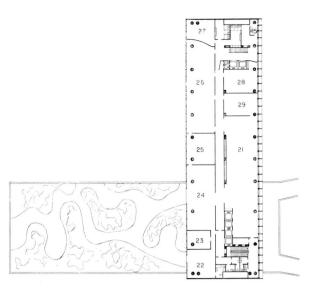

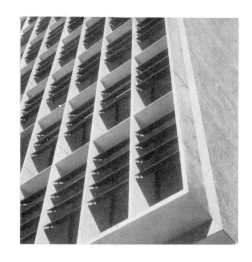

Third floor 1:1000

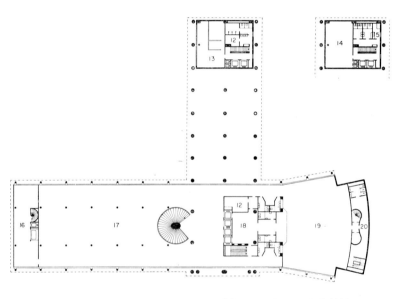

Second floor (Auditorium) 1:1000

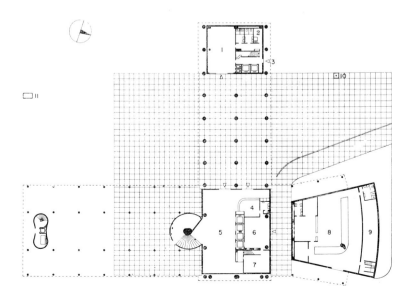

Ground floor 1:1000

ALVARO VITAL BRAZIL

Vital Brazil Institute / 1941 / Niterói, Rio de Janeiro

This building combines a scientific research center with an industrial laboratory for the preparation of biological and pharmaceutical products, and to this end, annexes have been added for workshops, cow-barns, stables, pigsties and pig-bleeding pens.

The general plan, not yet fully executed, is to include facilities for securing blood specimens from large animals, and performing operations and autopsies on them; an industrial pavilion, and museum lecture-room. There is to be a snake farm to ensure a regular supply of venom for the preparation of snake-bite serum, the manufacture of which dates back to Vital Brazil, the architect's father and a great Brazilian scientist.

The necessity for absolute sterility in the laboratories where the serums are prepared, bottled and packed, has resulted in a 'sealed' building, fully air-conditioned and equipped with a special system for accurately controling the purity, temperature and circulation of the air.

Nearly all the departments included in the program are laid out along the glazed southern façade of the three-story building raise on *pilotis*, while the access corridor runs along the northern on which is protected against excess sunshine by special fenestratio The stair-well and toilets, together with the main entrance, a contained in a tower abutting on the façade and extending ba over the flat roof to house the elevator machinery.

The first floor is given over to storage, display, and facilities f the personnel; the second comprises the manufacturing plant ar the third, the laboratories, while the fourth contains the admini trative offices and library in the west corner and a pen for 4 0C small animals on the east side. The water tank on the terrace ar the small windows cut in the main elevation make it easy to unde stand the sensation the building produced when the public fir saw it, with its direct, functional design and its uncompromising logical and disciplined shapes, in which the simplest elements reinforced concrete construction are successfully used to gi architectural character to a strictly utilitarian project.

Ground floor	Second floor	Third floor
1 Main entrance	19 Filtered air duct	36 Zootechnics
2 Check-room	20 Raw material	37 Bacteriology
3 Employees' entrance	21 Packing	38 Media preparation
4 Lockers	22 Cold storage, bottled products	39 Cold room
5 Mechanical equipment	23 Distribution	40 Warm room
6 Transformer	24 Distribution clerk	41 Animal bacteriology
7 Kitchen	25 Drying room	42 Biology
8 Director	26 Raw material autoclave	43 Sterile room
9 Storekeeper	27 Washing and sterilizing	44 Agitators and centrifuges
10 General storage	28 Cold storage	45 Precision scales
11 Receiving	29 Serum therapy	46 Culture examination
12 Crating	30 Agitators and centrifuges	47 Warm room
13 Stock room	31 Pharmaceutical products	48 Autoclave
14 Delivery	32 Gland products	49 Organic chemistry
15 Reception	33 Chemical products	50 Chemistry, director
16 Waiting room	34 Elevator	51 Inorganic chemistry
17 Examination	35 Cold room	
18 Clinic		

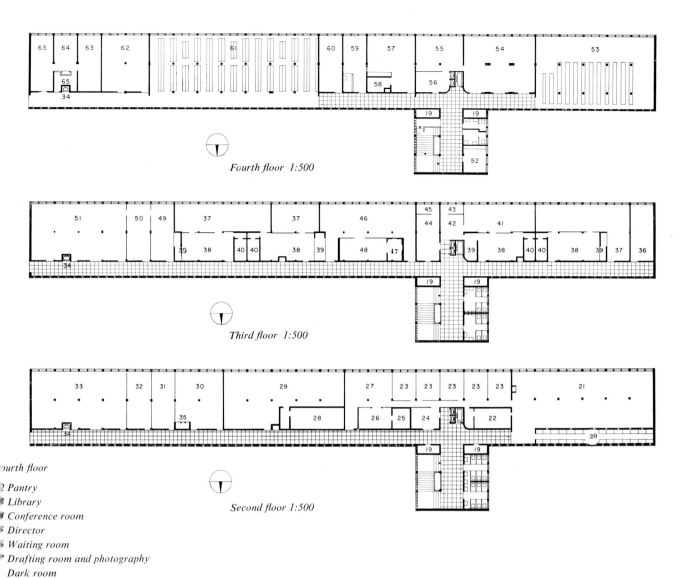

Fourth floor 1:500

Third floor 1:500

Second floor 1:500

...ourth floor

.. Pantry
.. Library
.. Conference room
.. Director
.. Waiting room
.. Drafting room and photography
.. Dark room
.. Rest room
.. Hydrophobia surgery
.. Animal quarters
.. Food preparation for animals
.. Animal isolation
.. Washing and sterilizing
.. Anteroom

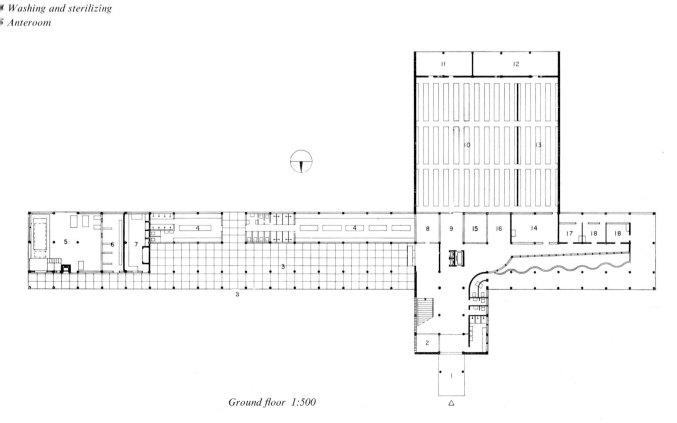

Ground floor 1:500

201

M. M. ROBERTO

Instituto de Resseguros do Brasil building / 1942 / Rio de Janeiro

This building was specially designed to house the Brazilian Reinsurance Institute, an organization created by the Federal Government in 1939, in which the capital is contributed jointly by the
State social security bodies (70%) and by the private insurance
companies (30%) in proportion to the capital of each.

The program covers not only space for management and office
staff, but also facilities for personnel instruction, social assistance
and recreation. Three elevators are assigned to the public, which
in no way interferes with the coming and going of the personnel,
for whom the other two elevators are exclusively reserved.

The plans reproduced here show the flexibility achieved in the internal layout by the use of an independent structure, and reveal the
concept of integral planning applied to a bureaucratic organism,
which traced the guiding lines as much for the institute itself as
for the building that was to house it.

The ground floor includes an open *pilotis* area for the public
entrance (reminiscent of the open portico of the A B I, but here
enriched by a handsome independent circular staircase leading to
the mezzanine), rental space for shops, entries for the personnel,
and a ramp leading to the underground garage.

The eighth floor, where the president's suite and the board rooms
are located, is essentially similar to the floors occupied by the
various departments. However, the president's office juts out from
the façade so as to stress the more important use to which this
floor is put. The toilets are grouped near the public elevators so as
to leave as much free space as possible for dividing up each floor
area according to the requirements of the various offices assigned
to it.

On the ninth floor, where the auditorium rises to a height of tw
stories, there is a bar, restaurant and lounge, as well as medic
services, a nursery and a library. These are roofed by a terra
with a garden designed by Burle Marx and a mural in mosaic t
by Paulo Werneck. A small bar is connected to the kitchen on t
lower floor. Access to the roof garden is provided by the ma
staircase, for the elevators could not be taken higher than t
auditorium level because of zoning regulations in the vicini
of Santos Dumont Airport which insist on hoisting machine
being kept within the maximum height of the building block.

The outer walls, made up of wooden structure and fiber-ceme
board sheathing, were pre-fabricated and assembled on the rei
forced concrete framework in 19 days. The inner partitions a
also pre-fabricated and can be taken down and set up aga
where required with the greatest ease.

The rooms on the north façade are protected by fixed vertical *bri*
soleil, consisting of pre-cast louvers of spongy concrete with
S-section so as to increase the efficiency of light reflection inwar
Louvers with three wooden battens are inserted in the cantilev
slabs supporting the *brise-soleil* at each floor-level so as to impro
the ventilation in the heat dispersion zone formed by the spa
between the *brise-soleil* and the plane of the windows.

The windows on the southern and eastern façades, which do n
require sun protection, are divided by a strip of fiber-cement in
two parts, the upper with swivel action and the lower with doub
hung sashes, thus avoiding the inevitable dazzle when panes r
from sill to ceiling.

1 *Public entrance*
2 *Garage entrance*
3 *Employees' entrance*
4 *Shop*
5 *Treasury*
6 *Vault*
7 *Treasurer*
8 *Board members*
9 *President*
10 *Waiting room*
11 *Office*
12 *Board room*
13 *Reception*
14 *Administrative assistant*
15 *Stenographers*
16 *Lounge*
17 *Medical services*
18 *Nursery*
19 *Reading room*
20 *Library*
21 *IRB Review*
22 *Auditorium*
23 *Men's lockers*
24 *Women's lockers*
25 *Kitchen*
26 *Bar*
27 *Projection booth*
28 *Mechanical equipment*

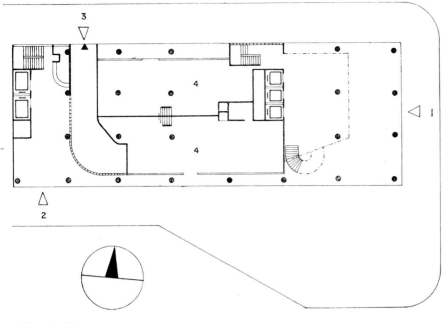

round floor 1:400

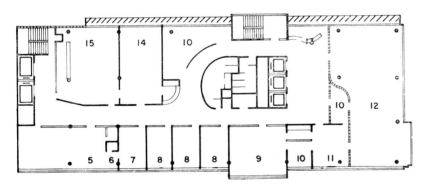

ghth floor (President's office) 1:400

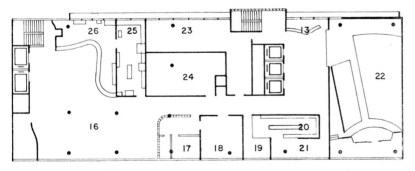

inth floor (auditorium) 1:400

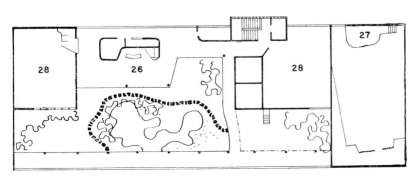

oof Terrace 1:400

203

EDUARDO KNEESE DE MELLO

'Leonidas Moreira' building / 1944 / São Paulo

The problems of ventilation and protection from the afternoon sun were solved in this small office building, designed in 1942, in an exceedingly straightforward, functional manner.

The façade markedly accentuates the reinforced concrete structure and is made up, in each module (corresponding to one room), of two panels of glass brick above and below a central panel of movable *brise-soleil*, with a small balcony separating this system from the glass doors behind it that form the outer wall of each room.

Unfortunately the glass brick comes out too dark in photograph and gives a poor idea of the lightness of the composition. Dra? in neat lines and two dimensions tempered by the relief of ? movable *brise-soleil*, this design is several years ahead of the smoo façades, composed simply of glass and framework, which, various fashions and so many places, have lately been bringing ? *fin-de-siècle* school of Chicago up to date and expressing the sa? fundamental ideas in modern terms.

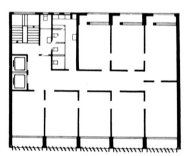

Typical floor 1:400

ree solutions to the problem of exposure, each equally straight-rward, have been incorporated in the exterior treatment of this ilding, erected primarily to hold the head offices of the Boavista nk. The southern façade, which gets practically no sun, is en-ely glazed and a happy effect is obtained by the reflection of ndelaria Church, located at the very beginning of Presidente rgas Avenue. The western façade, giving onto an extremely rrow street (Rua Teófilo Ottoni), is protected by vertical wooden *se-soleil*, movable so that they can be adjusted to the seasonal riation in the angle of the sun's rays. The back façade has a rthern exposure and here the classic solution of the Ministry Education building has been adopted; movable horizontal *se-soleil*, likewise of wood, are set into a pattern of horizontal d vertical reinforced concrete slabs. On the top floor, the uthern and western sides are partially protected to create a more timate environment for the employees' club, located on this floor. e color of the *brise-soleil* on the lateral façade merges from ite on the lowest floor (to increase the reflection of what little ht reaches the bottom of the canyon formed by the high buildings either side of the narrow street) to deep blue on the top floor ere the excess clarity needs to be tempered. Though this differ-ce in coloring produces a definite functional effect, it is barely rceptible from the street because of the compensating effect of e increase in luminosity at progressively higher levels. The lower ors, from the basement up to and including the fifth floor, are

occupied by the Bank, while the upper floors, from the sixth to the eleventh, are for rent. The twelfth, as mentioned, is used as a club by the employees of the Bank. The plans of the various floors, embodying the principle of a free structure independent of the walls, are laid out around an inner court which supplies light and air. Two separate groups of elevators and stairs are provided, one for the Bank and the other for the rented floors. Furthermore, in the Bank section the circulation of the public is kept separate from that of the personnel.

Outstanding features of the lower part of the buildings are the front portico (imposed by City regulations which call for a continu-ous sheltered sidewalk throughout each block, on either side of the avenue), and the vigorous treatment given to the glass brick wall winding along the side and back of the building. This wall, a re-markable example of the proper use of glass brick, is designed to produce a more stable surface than that obtainable with straight lines; not only does it enrich the outer and inner volume with special diversity in lighting effects, but it also makes for an ef-ficient arrangement of the area open to the public in the main hall of the Bank. On the mezzanine, which includes a waiting room with a large mural by Portinari, the offices of the management are supplied with glass walls to facilitate supervision of the ground floor.

The mosaic panel in the portico was designed and executed by Paulo Werneck.

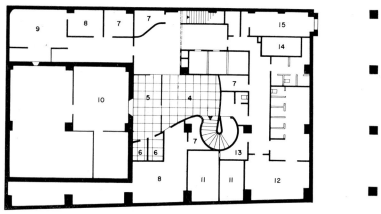

Basement 1:400

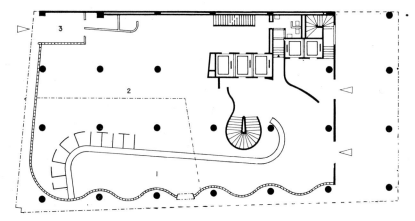

Ground floor 1:400

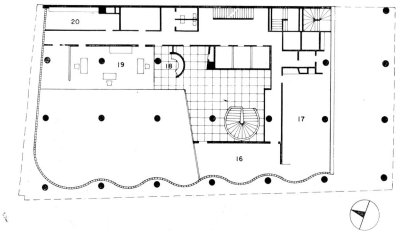

Ground floor mezzanine 1:400

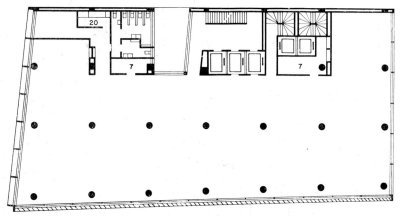

Typical floor 1:400

JORGE FERREIRA

Restaurant annex of the Oswaldo Cruz Institute (Manguinhos) / 1948 / Rio de Janeiro

This restaurant annex caters to one of the most important medical research institutes in the country, run by the National Health Department and located near Rio de Janeiro. It comprises two restaurants, each with a seating capacity of 150, for the white collar workers and a cafeteria seating 450 for the service personnel. Owing to the slope of the land, the back of the building with the cafeteria is at ground level, while the front where the restaurants are located is raised on *pilotis*. The kitchen occupies a convenient central position for serving both restaurants and cafeteria, and also has a counter opening onto the hall, from which trays are handed out to the cafeteria customers.

Access to the veranda in the front is provided by a ramp and by a lateral flight of steps. Adjoining the *pilotis* area, which is used rest and recreation after meals, are locker rooms for the resta rant staff, store-rooms and a boiler-room.

The elegance of the structure and of the main façade, enlivened *brise-soleil* on either side of the central rectangle of the wall and the ramp springing lightly from the ground, bears a striking co trast to the decoration of the paradoxical Moorish edifice built 1908, which houses the institute itself. The light touch whi distinguishes this interpretation of an essentially practical progra is a good example of the architect's contribution to the huma zation of environment.

1 Staff restaurant
2 White collar employees
3 Service personnel
4 Kitchen
5 Washroom
6 Food storage
7 Cold storage
8 Boilers
9 Incinerator
10 Storage
11 Not excavated

Lower floor 1:1000

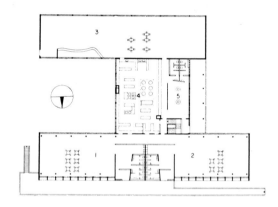

Upper floor 1:1000

ess utilitarian attitude towards a program that might appear
aspiring is also evident in the design of this small industrial
ding.

o parallel blocks, with work areas that can be subdivided at
, are connected by a corridor, along which locker rooms are
out on one side and accounting offices on the other. The mill-
k panels, simple in detail and inserted between the sidewalls
masonry, determine the character of the building, which takes

on a distinctive aspect in the graceful lines of the front porch of
reinforced concrete.

The two courtyards, facing opposite ways, provide a resting place
for the workers at various times of day.

It was originally intended to manufacture jewelry in this building,
but the simplicity of the design enabled it to be easily converted to
its present use as an aerophotogrammetric and air prospection
studio.

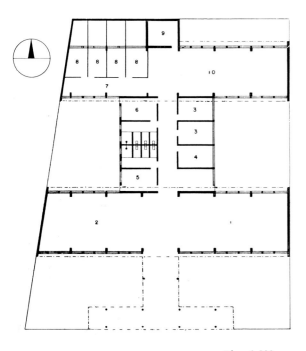

Plan 1:500

1 *Plane-table and drafting*
2 *Drafting and topography*
3 *Administration*
4 *Accounting*
5 *Men's lockers*
6 *Women's lockers*
7 *Technical photography*
8 *Photographic laboratory*
9 *Vault*
10 *Office of geology and aero-magnetism*

ABELARDO DE SOUZA, GALIANO CIAMPAGLIA, HELIO QUEIROZ DUARTE, JACOB RUCHTI, MIGUEL FORTE, RINO LEVI, ROBERTO CERQUEIRA CESAR *and* ZENON LOTUFO

Headquarters of the São Paulo Chapter of the Institute of Architects of Brazil / 1948 / São Paulo

This building, which is the headquarters of the São Paulo Chapter of the Institute of Architects of Brazil, is the outcome of a truly remarkable effort on the part of the Chapter, and in particular of its President at the time, Eduardo Kneese de Mello, who was largely responsible, both for the original idea and for the success achieved in carrying it out. The actual planning was done by a team, especially assigned to this project and selected by competition.

It comprises a basement rented to an artists' club, a store on the ground floor for displaying building materials, a double floor for the headquarters of the Institute, with a lecture room on the lower level and a lounge and restaurant on the mezzanine, topped by six floors of offices, sold under a cooperative ownership scheme and almost all occupied by architects.

Access to the office floors is entirely independent of the stairs lead-ing up to the headquarters of the Institute and down to the ba ment. Sub-division of the office floors is facilitated by the structu being independent of the façades and the location of the toilets two different points near the stair and elevator wells.

The setback of the windows on the two upper floors was desigr to comply with the Building Code regulations, which allowed floor slabs to be carried as far as the alignment as overhang sheltering purposes so long as they were not used as occupied are On the ground floor near the entrance there is a gaily color mural by Antônio Bandeira; in the headquarters of the Institu a magnificent mobile by Calder swings from the ceiling at a heig of 6 meters (19′ 8″)—as much a reminder of the artist's visit Brazil in 1948 as an example of the close connection between work and the spirit of modern architecture.

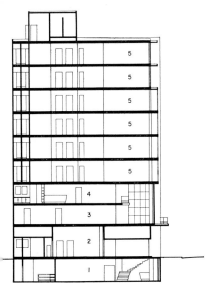

rtists' club
Main entrance
ecture room
lub lounge
ffices

ical floor 1:500

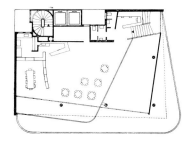

ond floor mezzanine 1:500

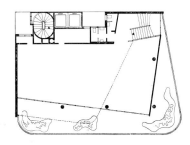

ond floor 1:500

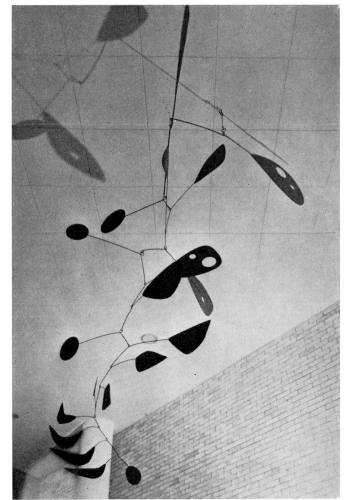

'Caramurú' building / 1946 / Salvador, Bahia

The recurrent problem of ensuring adequate protection against too much sunlight and heat has been solved here in a manner which merits a closer study.

Taking into consideration the warm climate of Bahia, its latitude (13° S.) and the exposure of the façades on two streets (enjoying a very fine view but requiring suitable protection all day long), the architect designed a system of light iron grilles 2 × 3 meters (6' 7¾" × 9' 10"), detached from the outer wall and arranged on two planes, alternating in checkerboard pattern, 25 cm. (10") apart, and resting on concrete brackets jutting out from the floor slabs. On these grilles a venetian blind made up of bronze strips 1 mm. (about 3/64") wide is stretched; this material ('Koolshade') is supplied by the makers in the form of a sort of wire gauze. The protection against excess sunshine thus obtained, as though by mosquito netting transformed into *brise-soleil*, is complete, without interfering with the view from the windows. At the same tim forms a peculiarly gay, forceful pattern on the façades, break up the monotony of the massive rectangular block.

The ground floor and mezzanine cover the whole area of the whereas the office block, seven stories high, is set back from lateral alignments so as to ensure ventilation and light on all sides.

The penthouse is used on inspection trips by the directors of São Paulo real estate company that owns the property. It sta in a roof garden atop the building and here a more capricious has been struck. Thus a copper wire composition by Mario Cr follows the rounded outline of the elevator hoist room; this cu is repeated in the wind-breakers of hollow cement block border the more intimate part of the roof-garden.

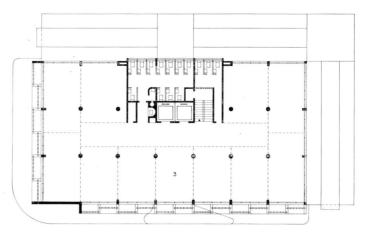

Typical floor 1:400

1 Shop
2 Mechanical equipment
3 Office space
4 Living-Dining
5 Bedroom
6 Kitchen

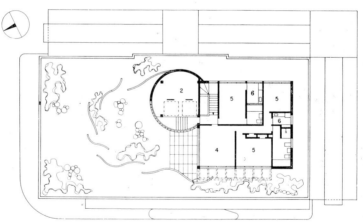

Roof terrace 1:400

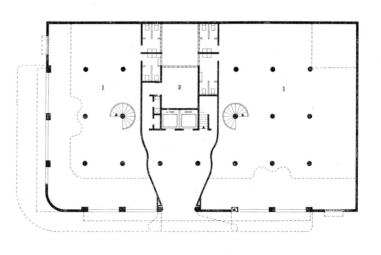

Ground floor 1:400

M. M. M. ROBERTO

'Seguradoras' building / 1949 / Rio de Janeiro

Here may be seen another variation of the basic systems of protecting excessively sunny façades. Whereas in the Caramurú Building (page 212) the venetian blind is reduced to its smallest possible slab width and thickness so as to combine shade on the façade with unimpaired visibility from the windows, in this building the same principle is adapted to large panels turning about a horizontal axis. The position of the panels can be regulated from inside the room so as to meet requirements at different times of day, and their size enables them to be set at some distance from the windows so as not to block the view. The hanging and regulating mechanism of these blinds is fixed to cantilever slabs at each floor level. The openings in the slabs, each corresponding to one of the venetian blinds and fitted with horizontal louvers, facilitate the circulation of hot air along the façade.

The basement, ground floor, mezzanine, and second floor (the latter served by independent elevators) are occupied by stores. T second floor windows, incorporated in the base of the buildi form a continuation of the ground floor display windows. T remaining floors, for offices, comprise a broad area along eit façade that can be partitioned with great flexibility according tenants' requirements, as the elevators, staircase, toilets and a conditioning plant are grouped in one central zone.

The curved wall connecting the glazed façade on the southeast face with the sun-screened façade on the other side of the buildi is faced with ceramic mosaic by Paulo Werneck, who also put the glass mosaic panels in the hall leading to the elevators. contrast with the ABI and Reinsurance Institute buildings design by the same architects, this edifice features a generous use of co (pink, grey, green, ochre and brown) in the treatment of façades, which gives them a cheerful appearance.

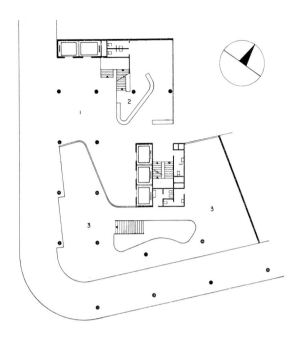

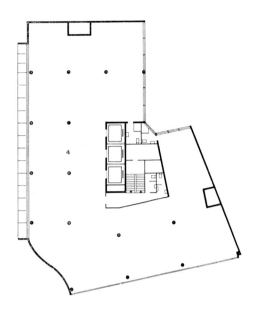

Entrance hall
Reception
Shop
Offices

Ground floor 1:500

Typical floor 1:500

M. M. M. ROBERTO

Industrial building for 'S O T R E Q' / 1949 / Rio de Janeiro

The variety of color in the preceding example is integrated in a much more complex interplay of masses in this building, designed to accomodate the showrooms, workshops and offices of the agents for Caterpillar tractors. It is located not far from the staff restaurant of the Oswaldo Cruz Institute (page 208).

The central part of the building is open to the public and contains the sales departments; the two wings in back of it, separated by a patio, house the spare parts warehouse and the workshops; to the front, there is a wing of offices laid out on either side of a long central corridor. The display areas extending outdoors are open and can be overlooked by customers, both from the overhead passageway and from the mezzanine in the central part. This glazed mezzanine, looking out onto the front garden and patio, contains the visitors' lounge, a restaurant, a small movie theater a lecture room.

The arches of laminated wood, anchored to reinforced concr pillars, have a span of 44 meters (144′ 4″) in the central part, meters (65′ 7″) in the rear wings (workshops and spare parts), a 12 meters (39′ 4″) in the office wing. Supporting the roof of fib cement, they form the basis of a composition dominated by middle arch painted in three colors: brown, white and black. Bel the arch, the glazed surface and the stone wall with the joi painted pink, contrast with the panel of vertical *brise-soleil* corrugated fiber-cement sheets painted pink and white, and, f ther, with the reinforced concrete canopy shading the worksho The millwork is painted pink, white and gray.

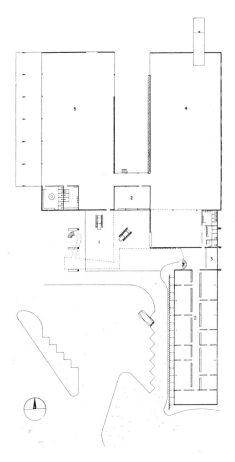

Ground floor 1:1000

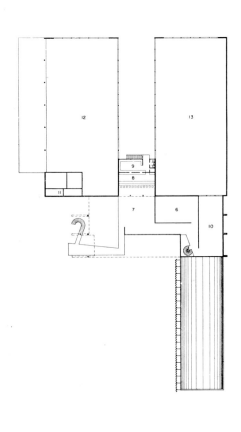

Upper floor 1:1000

Display
Offices
Reception
Spare parts warehouse
Workshops
Lecture room
Dining room
Pantry
Kitchen
Storage
Water tanks
Upper part of workshops
Upper part of spare parts warehouse

'Duchen' factory building / 1950 / São Paulo

In this design, also based on curving roof-lines, the structure, worked out by Joaquim Cardoso, is transformed into a daring investigation of the plastic possibilities of reinforced concrete.

The long building already finished forms part of a plant for manufacturing food products, located not far from São Paulo on the President Dutra Highway linking this industrial center to the city of Rio de Janeiro.

The overall layout, shown in the photograph of the model, is to include, on one side of the main block, a manufacturing unit (designed according to the same principles) and a small laboratory, and on the other, a two-story block for the administrative offices, a game room and a dining room, located beneath the free-shaped canopy and connected to a workers' swimming pool and to ex-

tensive landscaped recreation grounds. The structure of the m block, 300 meters (984') long, is made up of rigid reinforced c crete frames spaced 10 meters (32' 9¾") between centers, with spans of 18 meters (59') each, carrying the roof slab whic curved to improve the distribution of light. In the basement, workers' locker rooms are located near the entrance; on the treme right of the building, there is a first aid station. The su visor's office is on the glazed mezzanine, shown in the cr section, and from there he has a comprehensive view of the wl work area.

In the First São Paulo Biennial Exhibition, this project won prize in the industrial construction category.

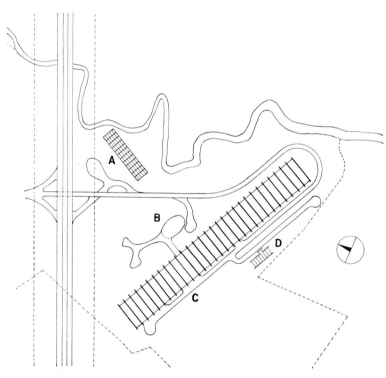

A Administration
B Restaurant
C Factory
D Laboratory

 1 Cold storage
 2 Fermentation
 3 Mixing
 4 Food products
 5 Biscuit
 6 Ovens
 7 Mechanical shop
 8 Reception
 9 Receiving and preparation of metal containers
10 Storage (empty containers)
11 Labeling and storage (paper and cardboard containers)
12 Storage and shipping of finished product
13 Carpenter shop
14 General storage

General site plan 1:5000

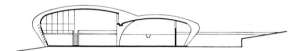

Section 1:1000

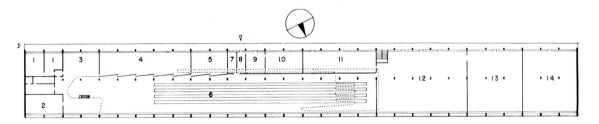

Plan of the factory 1:2000

ALVARO VITAL BRAZIL

'Banco da Lavoura' building / 1951 / Belo Horizonte, Minas Gerais

The triangular lot on which this building is constructed is typical of the central area of Belo Horizonte, planned in 1903 by Aarão Reis according to a rectangular layout crossed by long diagonals, revealing the influence of L'Enfant's plan for Washington, D.C. The shape of the site involved a difficult problem, which was solved by locating the elevators, stair well and toilets in the center of the plan, leaving all the surrounding area free to be divided up to suit tenants' requirements.

The buildings comprises a basement and sub-basement, and twenty-two floors above the ground floor, which has a ceiling height of 6 meters (19′ 8″). The basement, ground floor and first seven stories are occupied by the Banco da Lavoura. The other floors are rented as office space, with the exception of the top floor where there is a large lecture room. The sub-basement is taken up by machinery, water tanks, etc. A staircase for the public, with two flights, next to the ground floor entrance to the Bank, enables th basement to be used for departments dealing with the public. T reach the other floors, however, both tenants and customers of th Bank must take the same elevators, the use of the Bank's ow elevators being restricted to its personnel.

The façades, of clean-cut, sober design, correspond to the sim plicity and clarity of the layout and the structure. On the east sid the windows do not require any special protection, but on th northeast they are screened by movable vertical *brise-soleil* in as bestos cement; these are movable and the variation in positio according to the preference of the occupants in each room, giv the façade, thus subtly patterned, a great richness of texture.

Like the preceding project, this one was successful in the Firs São Paulo Biennial, carrying off the first prize for buildings fo commercial purposes.

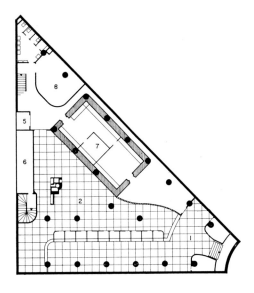

sement 1:400

1 Public hall
2 Clerks' work area
3 Waiting room
4 Manager
5 Personnel elevator
6 Elevator pit
7 Safe
8 Air conditioning
9 Office space
10 Ventilation well

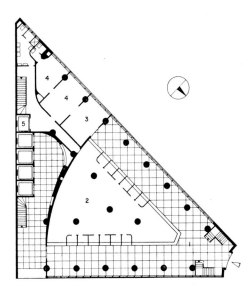

round floor 1:400

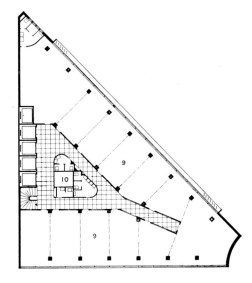

pical floor 1:400

Water tower (Factory of pharmaceutical products for Fontoura Wyeth S.A.) / 1953 / São Bernardo do Campo, São Paulo

This large plant for manufacturing penicillin and other pharmaceuticals, and the metal containers for them, was built with the joint collaboration of American and Brazilian technicians. Although skilled techniques of the highest order were involved and the most up-to-date details incorporated, the architect succeeded in unifying all the items on the program in a clear, well disciplined layout, significant of the high level of industrial developme[nt] demanded in the pharmaceutical field.

Special interest attaches to the neat, elegant design of the wa[ter] tower, protected by circular concrete rings which act as *brise-sol[eil]* and keep the temperature of the water down, thereby lesseni[ng] cooling expenses—an essential factor in this particular industry.

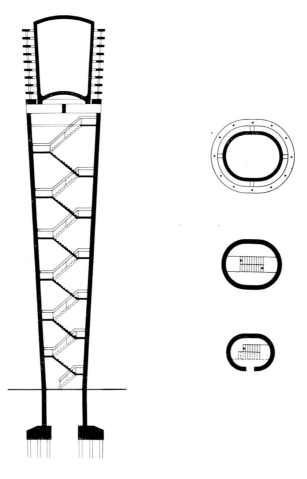

General view

Section and plan at different levels 1:400

Transportation, City Planning

Landscape Architecture

ATTILIO CORRÊA LIMA

'Estação de Hidros' (Seaplane station) / 1938 / Rio de Janeiro

This seaplane passenger station was planned by one of the pioneers of modern architecture in Brazil; ironically, it was not far from here that he met his death in a plane crash. But the building, his *chef-d'œuvre*, though not in use since the construction of the Santos Dumont Airport, lives on, for it is an example of first class design which does not seem to age, despite the passing of time.

The station was planned to group all the facilities for receiving and discharging passengers and luggage on the ground floor, while the upper floor was reserved for a restaurant opening onto the extensive observation terrace. A spiral staircase in the center of the layout connects the two floors and accentuates the wide open effect of the waiting area, which unifies the whole indoor space. A similar stair-case, smaller than the first, descends from the observation terr[ace] to the garden. A pathway, roofed by a light canopy carried [on] steel tubes, leads to the landing-stage and passengers arriv[ing] there used to be charmed by the tropical vegetation lining [the] path and running down to the water's edge, no less than by [the] gay plumage of the exotic birds in the aviary, one of the attra[c]tions of the garden.

The structure and the walls of the building itself are faced w[ith] travertine marble.

Architects Jorge Ferreira, Thomaz Estrella, Renato Mesquita d[os] Santos and Renato Soeiro collaborated in the project, which w[as] chosen by open competition (see page 6).

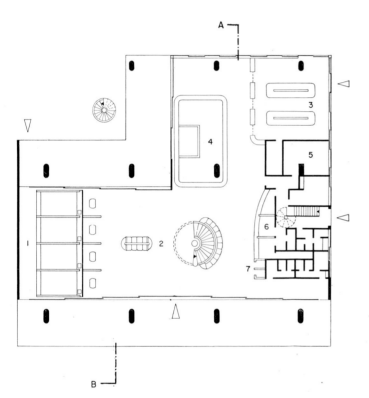

Ground floor 1:400

Upper floor 1:400

1 Baggage
2 Public hall
3 Customs
4 Administration
5 Pilots
6 Airline counter
7 Telephones
8 Restaurant
9 Kitchen-Pantry
10 Food and cold storage
11 Terrace

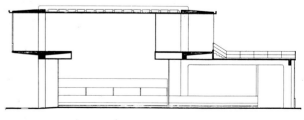

Section 1:400

CITY PLAN COMMISSION José de Oliveira Reis, *director*, Herminio de Andrade e Silva, David Xavier de Azambuja, Aldo Botel
Nelson Muniz Nevares, Armando Stamile Genarino, Edwaldo Moreira de Vasconcellos, *architects*

Master Plan for Rio de Janeiro / 1938-1948

This commission was formed in 1938 and in taking over the studies pursued by the French urbanist, A. Agache, from 1927 to 1930, and suspended in 1934, it sought to follow the guiding lines of the plan already prepared, while adapting them to the requirements deriving from the growth of Rio in the last twenty years.

The northern zone of the city is separated from the southern by a system of mountains, which means that connection between the two must be made through the center of town; this gives rise to overwhelming traffic difficulties. To solve the problem, the master plan now being carried out envisages: eleven tunnels, five of which are already in use (1, 2, 4, 5, and 6 on the plan); seven radial thoroughfares, of which three are open to traffic (E, O and N); and nine perimetral thoroughfares, only two in service as yet (A and L). The plan on the following page shows the central part of the city in greater detail, with, in the center of it, the area where Santo Antonio hill (page 232) is at present being leveled. The vertical to the right is the Avenida Presidente Vargas (N on the first plan), crossed (traveling from top to bottom) by the future perimetral avenue Cais do Porto-Copacabana (C), by the future North-South Avenue (B), by Rio Branco Avenue (A) and by the Perimetral Avenue (M), still to be completed. The shaded zone along the waterfront indicates the eventual extent of land now being reclaimed from the bay to improve traffic conditions along the Avenida Beira Mar (L) and create new public gardens and parking areas near the center of town.

The Avenida Presidente Vargas is to be provided with cover sidewalks on either side for pedestrians and to this end the f two floors of each new building must be set back the necessa distance, the overhang of the upper floors being supported b uniform row of columns running along close to the curb, so as form a continuous portico between street crossings when all t buildings are completed (page 205, Banco Boavista).

In the planning of this avenue, an interesting legal precedent w created. It was determined that the avenue was to be two c blocks in width, but instead of merely expropriating a strip of la two blocks wide to be cleared for the new thoroughfare, the C expropriated to a width of *four blocks*. The two lateral bloc after being grouped and redimensioned to fit in with a unifo plan, were put up for auction and sold for a price that grea exceeded the compensation paid for expropriation, on accou of the rise in land values due to the tracing of the new aven The profits of the operation, which went to finance the plan, th reverted to the City instead of going into the pockets of a hand of real estate owners as generally happens. Unfortunately, t zoning regulations originally enacted were altered under pressu of real estate lobbying to raise the maximum height from 15 to floors. This not only impaired the plan, but has also retarded execution, for a much heavier investment of capital is required the interested parties to erect the new buildings.

Main thoroughfares		
A Avenida Rio Branco	I Avenida Carioca	2 Pasmado
B Avenida Norte-Sul (North-South)	J Avenida Jacaré	3 Catumbí-Laranjeiras
C Avenida Cais do Porto-Copacabana	K Faria-Timbó Parkway	4 João Ricardo
(Docks-Copacabana)	L Avenida Beira-Mar	5 Rua Alice
D Avenida Rio Comprido-Lagôa	M Avenida Perimetral	6 Alaôr Prata
E Avenida Brasil	N Avenida Presidente Vargas	7 Rio Comprido-Lagôa
F Canal Parkway	O Avenida Rodrigues Alves	8 Uruguai-Jockey Club
G Avenida Radial Oeste (West)	P Avenida Portuaria	9 Andaraí
H Avenida Radial Sul (South)	Tunnels	10 Vila Izabel-Riachuelo
	1 Leme	11 Dois Irmãos

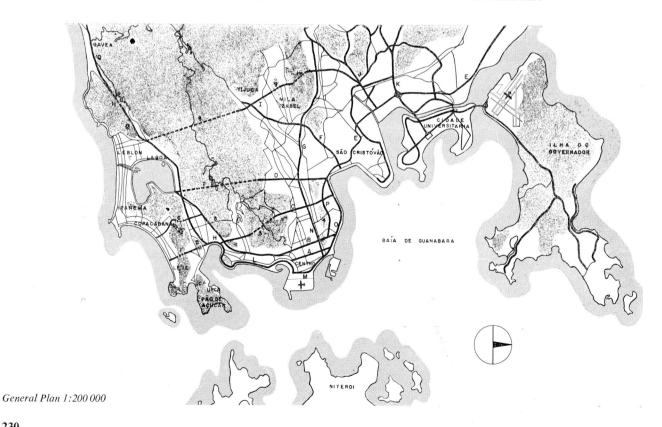

General Plan 1:200 000